Following God

for YOUNG ADULTS

REDEFINING NORMAL

A STUDENT DEVOTIONAL GUIDE
by
David Rhodes and Chad Norris

Following God:

REDEFINING NORMAL: Student Devotional Guide

Copyright © 2004 Wayfarer Ministries, Inc.

Published by AMG Publishers.

ISBN:0-89957-736-9

First printing: May 2004
Edited by: Robert Neely and Rick Steele
Graphic design: Jeff Belk at ImageWright Marketing and Design, Chattanooga, TN
Cover design: Daryl Phillips at ImageWright Marketing and Design

Wayfarer Ministries
Box 201
1735 John B. White Sr. Boulevard
Suite 9
Spartanburg, SC 29301-5462
864-587-4985

Printed in the United States of America

09 08 07 06 05 04 -C- 6 5 4 3 2 1
web sites: www.wayfarerministries.org   www.amgpublishers.com

To Our Parents

Table of Contents

REDEFINING NORMAL

For many of us, normal Christianity is comfortable and secure, isolated and based on all the evils we don't do. But what if our norm isn't normal to God? God isn't satisfied for us to settle for normal in our lives. He calls us to redefine normal as we get to know him better and learn more about his heart. God wants more than a church institution looking to protect the gospel in a fallen world. He wants a community of changed people reaching out to extend the gift of Christ and fulfill his redemptive purposes in the world he loves.

Redefining Normal challenges us to re-examine the norm in both culture and Christianity. Many of us have believed a half-gospel that says Christianity is all about what we don't do. The truth is there is much gmore to following God. God wants us both to celebrate the grace of God and to continue to grow in holiness. As we learn to live under the moral boundaries that God sets up for us, we also learn to focus on the postures of faith, hope, and love on which God wants us to center our lives. Through it all, we see God redeeming the world he loves and doing it through us.

Chad Norris and David Rhodes

Tips...
...on using this devotional book

This student devotional book is intended to help you redefine normal in your journey with Christ and lead you to a life of blessing, abounding in faith, hope, and love.

Some of you will be working through this study on your own, and some of you will be going through this study in a group. Either way, this book is designed to take truths that help us redefine normal in our lives and help us apply them to our daily lives. Our hope is that, if you've gone through the devotions during the week leading up to your group time, you will be able to share your thoughts with the group and build on the things you learned. If you are going through this study on your own, we hope that you will take some time to enter into discussions with your friends, family, and ministers about the things you are learning.

The book is divided into eight lessons with the purpose of allowing the reader to study one lesson per week for eight weeks. There are five devotional readings in each week. Although we have divided the devotions into a five-day schedule, feel free to create your own schedule for completing your study.

Recognizing that there is no perfect structure for time alone with God, we have tried to produce devotions that are both varied and consistent. This book provides stories, questions, illustrations, background information, graphs, and other tools to help illuminate the featured Scripture for each day and encourage and challenge your view of following God.

Each week's study concludes with a notes page. If you are taking this study with a group, we hope you will use this page to jot down notes during your group session. But if you are taking the study alone, you may want to use this page to journal your own personal highlights from the week.

We believe this study will help you grow in your understanding of God as you redefine normal, and we hope that you will have fun in the process. Let the journey begin.

REDEFINING NORMAL

NORMAL

CHALLENGING THE NORM

a fresh look
at being christian

what is
normal?

I have always loved summer. I think I love summer so much because so many of the things I enjoy happen in that time. School's out; ice cream is in. The days are long; bedtimes are later; curfews are extended. Life is sweet. But of all the things that summer brings, the one thing I looked forward to most as a child was spending my days at the pool. Kids by the thousands flock to swimming pools all over America like ants to a picnic. Some go to the pool to get a tan. Some show up at the pool to wrestle and play games in the shallow end. But more than anything else, the center of attention at the pool is the diving board.

Sadly, in our safety-first, lawsuit-driven world, fewer and fewer pools are willing to accept the liability of having diving boards. But in the special places that still have these pillars of fun, the ultimate is the high dive. Waiting to jump off the high dive is like waiting to go on a ride at Walt Disney World. The line stretches as far as the eye can see. The wait seems to take forever, but the magnetic pull of the rush you get when you jump from ten feet high is worth the wait. The high dive is the place where heroes are born and legends are made, the place where dreams are won and lost.

Once you stand on the high dive, you see what all the commotion is about. Ten feet doesn't seem that high from the ground when you're looking up. But from the top of the board, those ten feet seem to go on forever. When you reach the top, you realize the impact that could happen when you jump off— and then you have a choice to make. If you're a guy who carries a few extra pounds and is bigger than everyone else, you can go for the big splash. A good "cannonball," "can opener," or "preacher's seat" will send the whole pool into a fury. Others, however choose more death-defying options. These are the ones who have trained all year for just this moment. The hours spent practicing suddenly seem worthwhile as they leave the audience stunned with perfect back dives, "gainers" and the king of them all, the "one-and-a-half."

Still, there is another option. This option is one few choose but many stumble into unwillingly. This is, of course, the "belly flop." Most of the time this happens when someone attempts to stun the pool with a courageous dive only to rotate too far or too little and smack the water in a way to which everyone at the pool gasps in unison, "OOOOOH." A few oddballs will even pursue this option just to get such a response.

The older we get, the fewer options there are at the top of the high dive. It's one thing for a kid to smack the water, but when an adult does so, head trauma often results. Gone are the days of reckless abandon. The possibility of painful welts, bloodshot eyes, and a frightening lack of feeling are enough to take the recklessness of childhood away—at least until someone levels a double-dog dare. Not too long ago, this scenario played out with my friends and me. We dared each other to attempt the prized "one-and-a-half," which none of us had tried since the days of our youth. So we daredevils trudged (albeit hesitantly) to the high dive, promising to fling our bodies toward the water if the rest of the group promised to do the same.

This time, instead of getting encouragement from the rest of the pool-goers, our wives stood in the shallow end, begging and pleading for us to regain some semblance of sanity and chicken out of this stunt. But not wanting to be told what to do, we went to the high board one at a time. The first guy nailed the "one-and-a-half," leaving everyone mesmerized by his courage. (Can I tell you that I was this brave soul?) The second guy, full of passion, miscalculated his jump and smacked the water. That made the threat of pain all the more real to everyone watching. Then the third guy made his way to the top of the board. He tried to talk himself into doing what he had promised to do. He had seen one guy nail the "one-and-a-half" and bask in all the glory. He had seen the other poor soul smack the water with a body-jarring, mind-numbing "THWHACK!" and come up violently gasping for air. The third guy wanted to risk everything and outdo the first two contestants; yet, something held him back. He was so afraid of messing up that, when he finally got the courage to jump, instead of flipping, he turned into a pencil and went feet-first into the water. Of course, this moron was showered with a chorus of boos by the same wives who earlier were pleading with their husbands to temper their testosterone levels and abort this dangerous stunt. His own wife led this cacophony of critics by calling him a chicken. So, this glutton for punishment stepped back up on the high dive, only to remain frozen again. He just couldn't seem to talk himself into the risk.

Many of us stand in a similar position in our Christian lives. We are so afraid of messing up that we are convinced God's great goal for our lives is for us to just say "No" to everything. We believe the only thing God is interested in is "pencil dives" and that a good Christian is one who doesn't do anything to make waves.

The question of *Redefining Normal* is whether this just-say-no society we have created is the same movement that Jesus had in mind when he came to earth. Is Christianity only about setting moral boundaries, or could purity far outweigh those boundaries?

Read Luke 4:14-21

■ In your own words, write Jesus' mission as stated in verses 18-19.

_____

_____

_____

■ Which does Jesus' mission sound more like?
  ❑ the "pencil" dive
  ❑ the "one-and-a-half" dive

■ Which of the following words would you use to describe Jesus' purpose statement in these verses?
  ❑ safety
  ❑ change
  ❑ the status quo

Jesus shows us that Christianity is more about saying, "Yes," than it is about saying, "No." It is more about risk than safety, more about change than the status quo. The change Jesus longs to trigger in our lives is nothing less than revolutionary. This book is a journey toward a revolution of the soul. Today, we start the path to waking up to life as God intends it. If we will be willing to take risks over the next eight weeks, we will find that God has more in mind for us than lame pencil dives.

Take some time to write a description of what you think a mature Christian looks like. After you have written your description in the space below, ask God to help you in your understanding, to encourage you in the places you are right and to correct you in places where you are still learning. (We all have areas in our lives where we are still learning.) Then ask God to use this study to help you see the kind of life he intends for you to have.

_____

_____

_____

_____

_____

_____

the story
part one: beauty

As we journey toward life as God intends it, we must begin by understanding our story as Christians. We can only embrace what we recognize. So over the next few days, we will spend some time becoming more familiar with God's redemptive story. The four words we will use as mileposts for this story are beauty, broken, baptism, and blessing. Today we begin the story by looking at beauty.

Read Genesis 1-2

■ **What thoughts strike you most as you read these chapters?**

_____

_____

_____

_____

_____

■ **How did God evaluate the world he made?**
- ☐ very bad
- ☐ bad
- ☐ OK
- ☐ good
- ☐ very good

■ What does God's evaluation of the world at creation tell you about the world we live in today?

_____

_____

_____

_____

■ How would you describe the role of man and woman in the Garden of Eden?

_____

_____

_____

_____

I am not an artist, but I appreciate those who are. My home is filled with pottery and paintings my wife has made. While she always blushes in embarrassment when I mention her work to people who visit our house, our home is much better off because of her artistic nature. If decorating were up to my artistic ability, the paintings on our walls would be nothing but stick figures.

Most artists I know are pretty bashful about their work. Something must truly be good to get their seal of approval. Much of the time they feel as though even their greatest works are still to some degree incomplete. But imagine an artist emerging from her studio with a piece of art that was not only so complete that any addition would diminish it but also was the favorite piece she had ever created. Picture the spark of electricity coming from her eyes every time it was displayed. The pride and sense of accomplishment that piece embodied would be the way the artist would want to be remembered forever.

While God is certainly more than a good artist, I think we walk away from Genesis 1 and 2 with a thought similar to the illustration above. God values his work of creation as very good. It is his masterpiece. It is the work that declares who he is, a work to which he is heavily attached. The word **beauty** seems like an understatement when we look at God's world as he created it. Even after all this time, whenever we watch a sunrise or sunset, gaze at the stars at night, climb up a mountain and catch a glimpse of its majesty, see a humpback whale come up for air, or watch a tree blossom in the first days of spring, we stand amazed at the beauty of God's world.

So what is our role? In the Garden of Eden, the first man and woman were what we could call stewards of beauty. God discharged his authority to Adam and Eve in much the same way that an employer discharges authority to his apprentice or assistant. God created the world—and man and woman—in the image of God. Adam and Eve were appointed the vice presidents of operations. Their days were filled with work and purpose. Their walks with God in the cool of the day functioned as board meetings. Life was good. This is life as God intended it.

prayer exercise:

Plan to take some time during the next twenty-four hours to watch a sunrise or sunset. Settle in during this time. Watch the sun dip below or rise above the horizon and bask in the afterglow or early flashes of light that appear even when the sun is nowhere to be seen. Let the glow of light minister to you as you remember how, in much the same way, we live in the afterglow of creation. Marvel at the beauty that is around you today.

the story
part two: broken

I have what you might call a spilling issue. For as long as I can remember, I have dropped food, spilled drinks, and knocked over fragile items. It's not that I want to spill, but maybe because of my tendency to overlook details, spilling just seems to come naturally to me. In fact, just a few days before I sat down to write this devotion, I did it again. After a hard day of working in the yard digging holes and planting bushes, I settled down on the couch to watch a little college football. I assured my wife that, as a grown-up, I could handle eating my dinner away from the kitchen table. I had been to a Sonic™ drive-in to pick up a hamburger, some jalapeño poppers and a big soft drink. This soft drink wasn't a medium, large, or even extra large size. It was the size they had to come up with a new name for—the "Route 44."® But just minutes after I sat down to eat, my Route 44® drink was all over the living-room carpet. In one of those moments that seem to happen in slow motion, I picked up the cup from the top only to feel it break and slip away. I dove to catch it and prevent the spill, but it was no use. Soda and ice were everywhere.

It would be one thing if this were the only time something like this had happened to me. But whether it was a cup, my mom's Precious Moments™ figurines or my wife's pottery, it seems as though I can't go anywhere without breaking something. Every time it happens, I confidently think I will never do it again. But before I know it, I find myself on the floor trying to clean up another mess I've created.

■ What is the biggest spill you can
remember causing?

_____

_____

_____

■ How did you feel when the spill happened? (Check all that apply)

- ☐ horrible
- ☐ anxious
- ☐ clumsy
- ☐ sorry
- ☐ guilty
- ☐ foolish
- ☐ childlike
- ☐ exposed

Read Romans 1:18-32

■ Using twelve words or less, put Paul's thoughts from this passage in your own words.

_____

_____

_____

When the apostle Paul looked around at the world and people in it, he saw more than beauty. The word **broken** can't fully describe what Paul saw, but it begins to paint the picture. Paul saw creation, but he also saw sin, depravity, and, to put it mildly, people living second-rate lives. The fingerprints of Romans 1 can be traced back to Genesis 3. In the biggest spill of all time, Adam and Eve ate of the one tree (the tree of the knowledge of good and evil) from which God told them not to eat. Needless to say, we human beings have been in a downward spiral ever since. Just as I have broken cups, ceramic figurines, and countless plates, the sin of Adam and Eve shattered God's beautiful creation. The pieces left scattered on the ground now tell two stories, one of beauty and one of brokenness.

It would be one thing if the Fall ended in the Garden of Eden. But day after day, the fall continues in our own lives. The broken pieces continue to be broken into even smaller pieces. Though the Bible primarily conveys a story of hope, its pages also feature many broken lives. From Cain to the people of Noah's time, from Noah himself to the construction of the Tower of Babel, and on and on, a story of brokenness continues, stretching even into today. Now, it seems as though brokenness rules the day. We need only read a newspaper, watch the news, or open our eyes to the world around us to see the things we have broken and the broken lives sin has caused us to live.

From terrorism, to global warming, to divorce, it seems at times as though the world is spinning out of control.

Adam and Eve responded to their spill in much the same way we often respond to our spills. They hid, ashamed of their sin, their nakedness and their destruction of God's good creation. When God came calling, their fear, anxiety and feelings of foolishness took them into the shadows. The shadows continue today as well. All over the world, people are hiding from God. We may not call it hiding. We may say we are seeking our own way or doing our own thing or living life to the fullest. But in the end, we are left alone, staring in the mirror face-to-face with the ramifications of the second-rate lives we are living.

prayer exercise:

Use the space below to write down some of the spiritual spills you have made in your life. Take some time today to evaluate the brokenness those spills have brought to your life and the lives of those around you. Then spend some time watching the news on TV, looking for stories of brokenness. Ask God to help you have a realistic view of the brokenness around you.

_____

_____

_____

_____

the story
part three: baptism

The stories of beauty and brokenness are all around us. Often, the seeming contradiction between the two has left us to wonder what purpose and meaning life has. For centuries, philosophers, poets, and spiritual leaders have tried to make sense of a world where beauty and brokenness co-exist. Christianity is not immune to this problem. In fact, Christianity's honesty about the stories of beauty and brokenness can make it appealing to seekers of truth. God created the world as good; that is why we see beauty. Man and woman walked away from God in sin; that is why we see brokenness. Although we understand this story, we still wonder, "What now?" No reasonable discussion of why beauty and brokenness exist will solve the longings in our heart. There remains deep inside of all of us the cry to find our way home, back to the beauty of the Garden.

Baptism is the word that illustrates this journey back to the Garden. The type of baptism we're discussing today is figurative in nature. We will not discuss the act of being immersed or sprinkled in front of a church. Instead, we're using a more generic definition of baptism to paint a picture of life through death. Baptism celebrates the possibility of change. Brokenness need not be the end or overarching characteristic of our lives, because, although we are fallen and shattered, God has picked up the pieces.

> Read Psalm 40

■ What word best describes David in this passage?
- ☐ helpless
- ☐ numb
- ☐ prideful
- ☐ powerful

- What word best describes God in this passage?
  - ☐ removed
  - ☐ distant
  - ☐ apathetic
  - ☐ deliverer

- Put Psalm 40 in your words in twelve words or less.

_____

_____

If you have ever broken a bone, you know the pain of brokenness. As an eighth grader, I broke my collarbone playing basketball. I remember the utter sense of helplessness I felt as I laid on the gym floor. I had taken hits before. Each time, I had been able to get back up. But this time, my body wouldn't move. I could not fix myself. I needed a doctor. I was broken.

Sin has left us in a similar predicament. We are sinners, not just because Adam and Eve sinned but because we sin as well. As sinners, we are left broken spiritually with no one to blame but ourselves. In need of the Great Physician, we can only wait for the stretcher and the ambulance and hope that he will be able to reset the broken pieces and heal us.

The good news of the Bible is that God is not removed, distant or uncaring. He has moved for us in the middle of our brokenness. God has picked up the pieces, first by creating a chosen people through Abraham and then by sending his only son, Jesus, through this people to deliver us from brokenness. We learned in the first day of the study that change was Jesus' mission statement. The story of the New Testament is that Jesus has stepped into our world and proclaimed, "Let all the broken pieces come to me. I will put you back together." Then he died, taking our brokenness upon himself. Three days later, he was resurrected from the dead, conquering brokenness for us. Now we, too, can enter into his resurrection when we come to the end of ourselves, ask for help and place our faith in him. Baptism is the word picture that describes this monumental resetting of the broken pieces of our lives. While this will hurt, and it may take some time for us to function normally, God's work of restoration is released in us at the moment of salvation.

Psalm 40 is David's cry in the midst of his desperation. He sensed God's deliverance in the past and here cried out for God to continue his work of deliverance. Use your prayer time today to cry out to God for deliverance as well. If you have come to God through salvation, thank him for that. If you have not, take some time now to offer your life up to Jesus and ask him to deliver you from your sin. Spend the rest of your prayer time reflecting on the ways he has delivered you from brokenness. You may want to play a worship CD to help you meditate on this life-altering truth.

the story
part four: blessing

Genesis
12:1-4

Over the past century, there may not be a city in the world that has been more marked by world events than Berlin, Germany. Berlin was a primary player in two World Wars, and the city carries the scars to prove it. At the end of World War II, the city was in ruins. Then the city was divided in half. For more than forty years, the Communist bloc controlled East Berlin, and the Western world controlled West Berlin. A twelve-foot wall ran through the city and separated the two sides. The Berlin Wall was a stark reminder of the Cold War and the tension between the U.S.S.R. and U.S.A. The architecture on both sides of the wall highlighted the differences as well. West Berlin modeled itself after Los Angeles, while East Berlin modeled itself after Moscow. Tension grew as the world's two superpowers maneuvered for control not only of Berlin but also of the entire world, and it sometimes looked as though only a nuclear holocaust would break the stalemate. But times eventually changed in Berlin—not because of nuclear war, but because something on the inside was working its way out. Communism was collapsing from the inside. And in a moment of great historical significance, the wall came down on November 9, 1989.

If you travel to Berlin today, you can still see the distinction between sides of the city. While massive restructuring programs are going on, some visitors have said that much of the architecture still tells a tale of division and separation. And there are historical markers and monuments where the wall once stood. In one of these places hangs a mural that reads, "Many small people who do many small things in many small places can change the fate of the world." (Citation: Matt Williams, "Berlin: Untangling the Past," *World Traveler*, July 2003) The change in Berlin, and in our entire world, didn't happen through bombs; it happened in the hearts and minds of individuals. I think this mural captures the truth of **blessing** perfectly.

The thing that impresses me most about God is not creation. While the beauty I encounter every day often overwhelms me, it rarely stretches my imagination to think of God creating the world out of nothing. I expect the miraculous from God. What blows my mind is that God creates good from bad.

Even more, I'm surprised that he calls us to join him in this job of re-creation.

■ **How has God created good from bad in your life?**

_____

_____

_____

■ **How has God used you to create good from bad in someone else's life?**

_____

_____

_____

Many people stop developing the story of their lives at the place we stopped yesterday. For them, baptism (gaining life through death) is the ultimate goal. Sadly, Christianity to many is just about salvation. Once they are in the Christian tent, nothing else really matters. Others feel there must be more, but because they don't understand God's purpose or mission in this world, they spend their days merely trying to make a clear distinction between those who are Christian and those who are not. Tragically, this distinction often becomes nothing more than behavior management, and the Christian's mission becomes the life of "No." Pencil dives rule the day. This is the kind of world into which Jesus came. The ruling Pharisees were a sect bent on distinguishing the true Israel. Because of Israel's past failures—due to the nation being influenced by a broken world —the Pharisees decided the best way to make sure Israel fulfilled God's purposes was to manage everyone's behavior. To put it in the analogy we used on the first day, Israel had been kicked out of the pool for diving in the shallow end, and the Pharisees tried to solve the problem by hanging a big "No Diving" sign. The way they made sure they didn't fall into the world's trap again was through distancing themselves from the world. You can see why Jesus got into trouble when he told the Pharisees they were missing the point by going to an opposite extreme from their ancestors. Even more, you can see the flips and dives for which Jesus was crucified—ministering to sinners, healing the lame, and proclaiming the year of the Lord's favor.

If we are honest about the monumental change we have experienced, I think we will admit there is something within us calling us to more than pencil dives. **We are not called away from the world but to it**. While we are often paralyzed by fear, we long to flip and dive, to pick up Jesus' mission as our own just as the disciples did in the years after Jesus' ascension to heaven. Blessing calls us toward this end.

"Blessing" is the word we're using to describe life after salvation. We mean more than "being blessed." Blessing describes the kind of lives we are to live. We, as Christians, are called to be a blessing to our world. To understand this mission, we must journey back to the beginning and understand God's calling to one of the fathers of our faith.

Read Genesis 12:1-4

Fill in the blanks:
Genesis 12:3 says, "I will bless those who bless you, and whoever curses you I will curse; and _____ on _____ will be _____ through _____."

■ What was God's call to Abram?

_____

_____

Two commands structure Abram's calling. The first is to go forth: "leave your country" (verse 1). The second is "be a blessing" (verse 2). While we lose the impact of this message in many English translations, what God was calling Abram to do was to go forth to be a blessing. Here is the essence of following God in a few words. We are people on a journey, and that journey leads us to be blessings for our world.

Before this point, the story of the world had been dominated by brokenness. Adam and Eve had fallen and started a downward spiral in which Cain stumbled, followed by the people of Noah's day, and even Noah himself. The downward spiral continued as the Tower of Babel was being erected, when men and women tried to build a structure of their own to reach to heaven. It was a dismal failure. Yet God was implementing a plan for the human race that no men or women could enact for themselves. This plan made the way for humanity to come back home. Part of this plan called for one chosen man, Abram, to do the unthinkable—leave his home country and journey to a place he would only know when he got there. He had no map or directions. Abram was simply to leave and trust that God would guide his steps. As Abram journeyed, God would take his faith and bless the world through it. While the world was still falling, one chosen man began to travel in a different direction. Of course, Abram would still struggle with sin, but the defining characteristic of his life was not falling but faith and, ultimately, blessing. Through Abram, God created a nation. Through this nation, the Messiah was born. Through this Messiah and his followers, the world is being redeemed.

Redefining Normal is about bridging the gap from baptism to blessing in our lives. We'll look at Christianity as more than a set of behaviors we avoid. We'll understand that we have been changed for a mission and that we are to further the calling Jesus assumed in Luke 4. God has called us to be part of his re-creative work in the world. Christians are people who, as they journey home themselves, also bring home to their journey. We are people who are not separate from the world but separate for the world.

prayer exercise:

Use the chart on the next page to help you understand the continual story of beauty, brokenness, baptism, and blessing in the life of Israel. Once you have looked at it, take some time to chart your own spiritual journey in the space below. Your chart probably looks a lot like Israel's journey. Notice the way that God continues to deliver even when his people fall. Notice the times that Israel and you have joined him in this re-creative work. Thank God for calling you to be a blessing to the world.

a history of God's people

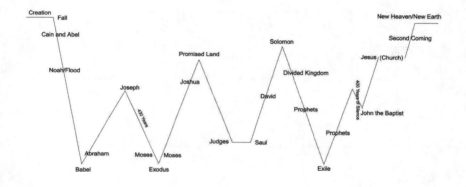

Creation
Fall
Cain and Abel
Noah/Flood
Babel
Abraham
Moses
430 Years
Joseph
Moses
Exodus
Judges
Joshua
Promised Land
Saul
David
Solomon
Divided Kingdom
Prophets
Prophets
Exile
400 Years of Silence
John the Baptist
Jesus (Church)
Second Coming
New Heaven/New Earth

_____

_____

_____

_____

_____

_____

_____

_____

_____

_____

_____

_____

_____

_____

This page is designed to give you space to take notes during your "Redefining Normal" group session or to journal your reflections on the highlights of this week's study.

REDEFINING NORMAL

STARTING POINT

rooted in grace

living in
grace

Doug has a problem. Every time he learns something new, he forgets it almost immediately—just like Dory, the fish who suffered from short-term memory loss in the recent Disney film, *Finding Nemo*. Doug isn't sure where his memory problem came from or why he has it. If you ask him why he doesn't remember something, all he can say is, "I don't know. I guess if something's not that important, I don't remember it."

But there are some things that Doug has no problem remembering. He loves football, and he can quote the statistics and records of all his favorite teams. He loves his car, and he can tell you anything you want to know about the differences between makes and models of cars. He loves to eat out, and he can tell you the best thing to get at every great restaurant within an hour's drive. Doug remembers these things. It's the other things life offers that give him trouble.

■ Do you ever feel as though you have a short-term memory problem when you are reading the Bible?

❏ yes
❏ no

If so, describe that situation.

_____

_____

_____

_____

_____

■ Do you sometimes have to hear a truth from God's word more than once before you get a good grasp of it?

❑ yes
❑ no

Give an example from your life.

_____

_____

_____

Read Colossians 2:6-15

Fill in the blanks:
Colossians 2:6 says, "So then, just as you _____ Christ Jesus as _____, _____ to _____ in him."

There is so much meat in this verse. Paul is telling us to walk in Jesus just as we received him. What does this mean? First, we must understand what it means to receive Jesus. You can look back to at the picture of baptism from last week to be reminded of this. Think back to the time when you called upon the Lord for salvation. Remember what your life was like at that point. Can you remember how lost you were in your sin? You recognized that you were living a life apart from God and that you needed him to forgive you. You called out to your Jesus, and he saved you.

As we think back to what happened when we were saved, we see that we did not offer the Lord anything. He offered salvation as a gift, and we received it. We are saved by grace through faith (Ephesians 2:8). Most of us understand grace at salvation, but often we fail to remember to live by grace.

■ Write out your definition of grace.

_____

_____

■ What do you think it means to walk
   or live by grace?

_____

_____

_____

The powerful message in today's passage is that we aren't just saved by grace; we live by grace as well. In other words, God loves you unconditionally **at this very moment**. He loved you when he saved you, and he loves you now. You will never be able to satisfy his righteousness with your actions. Only the work of Jesus on the Cross can do that. But when we believe in Christ, God looks at us with love and grace. The starting point of redefining normal is the truth that we must be rooted in grace. Just as a golfer must address the ball properly to hit a good shot or a basketball player must be lined up to make a free throw or musician must have the right posture to play an instrument well, we must be set up in grace if we are to pursue a life of blessing. This is a message we need to speak to ourselves every day. Grace was present when we came to Christ, and grace is present now. We are saved by grace through faith, and God calls us to live the same way.

prayer exercise:

Ask God to reveal to you what it means to live in Christ just as you did when you received him. This message is one that we need to hear over and over, because it's so easy for us to forget. To help this message sink in, spend some time reminding yourself of God's message. Say the following truths out loud: "I am loved and accepted by God. Grace was present when I was saved,

and it's present now. I am completely loved by God. My actions
alone will never please him. My
faith in what his son did for me is
what pleases him." Once you've
reminded yourself of these truths,
take a few moments to enjoy being
with your Father who loves you.

what's your focus?

When Janet visited the Louvre Museum in Paris, she could not wait to see the *Mona Lisa,* a painting known throughout the world. I've seen people weep at the sight of this beautiful portrait (even though I think she looks kind of miserable). Once they entered the museum, Janet and her mom made a beeline toward the room that housed the painting. There was a huge wait, because so many other people were as anxious as Janet to see this masterpiece. When Janet finally got to the front of the line, she was awestruck. She had seen pictures of this painting all her life but had never imagined how beautiful it would be in person. It was worth the wait.

Later that evening, Janet and her mom were eating dinner at a nearby restaurant when a well-known artist walked in. Janet's mom knew enough about art to recognize this artist as the designer of several sculptures that were housed in famous museums. Janet's mom pointed this artist out, and Janet went up to ask for his autograph. Janet told him that she had been at the Louvre that day. So he asked her, "Did you see my work?" She asked him where it was, and he said it was in the same room as the *Mona Lisa.* Janet became embarrassed. She had to admit that she hadn't noticed his sculpture because she was so focused on the *Mona Lisa.* Janet was disappointed that she had missed this famous artist's work, which had been only a few feet away.

■ **What are you focused on? (Check all that apply)**

❑ school   ❑ job
❑ family   ❑ money
❑ boyfriend/girlfriend   ❑ sports
❑ possessions
❑ other_____

■ **What happens when we are so focused on other things that we miss the work of God's grace in our lives?**

_____

_____

_____

■ Has that ever happened to you?
❑ yes
❑ no

We are people consumed with a few things. Most of us have one or two things in our lives that take up all our focus and time. Students are focused on school, while parents are focused on their children and work. People spend enormous amounts of time staring at the Mona Lisas of their lives, and they miss the other art all around them. This happens with God as well. Christians who struggle with feelings of condemnation and guilt spend their time focusing on how unfit they are for the love of God. That might not be your focus, but we've all been in similar situations. We struggle with a sin we can't kick, gossiping about someone when we know it's wrong and doing whatever it takes to gain in popularity or prestige.

The bottom line is that we are far too focused on ourselves. This is very dangerous when it comes to our relationship with God. When we constantly focus on how sinful we are or how often we fall short of God's plan for us, we get trapped in the black hole of guilt and condemnation. The remedy is to change our focus.

Read Psalm 27

David was running for his life when he wrote this psalm. He was desperately in search of a shelter. In verse 4, he stepped into the shelter of God, and what he saw there brought peace in the middle of chaos.

As you read this passage, focus on the word "gaze" in verse 4 (NIV). Picture Janet gazing at the _Mona Lisa_. To gaze at something is to give it complete concentration, to stare at it. If you are struggling with living in God's grace, fix your gaze on something beyond yourself. Stare at God and concentrate on his character. Take your focus off yourself.

■ What are some things you can do to take your focus off yourself?

_____

_____

■ What are some things you can do to put your focus on God?

_____

_____

prayer exercise:

Close this time with God by focusing on how good he is and how much he loves you. One of the best things you could ever do is to open yourself up to God. Come before him with an honest and sincere heart today. If you are struggling to accept his love and grace for you, tell him about it. Use the space below to write a prayer expressing your love for God and your desire to be rooted in grace.

_____

_____

_____

_____

_____

_____

seeing as
God sees

Have you ever thought about what God sees when he looks at you? In my work, I talk to a lot of people about God, and I have come to realize that most believers have no idea what God sees when he looks at them. Some people aren't sure, and those who are sure believe that God sees wretchedness, sin, and filth in them. But in his word, God tells us we are destroyed by a lack of knowledge (Hosea 4:6). People of God all over the world are dying slow deaths emotionally because of their ignorance about what God sees in his children.

■ **What do you think God sees when he looks at you?**

_____

_____

_____

_____

■ **Do you ever struggle with your self-worth and confidence?**

☐ yes
☐ no

If so, how? If not, why not?

_____

_____

_____

■ How does your belief about what God sees in you impact this struggle?

_____

_____

_____

When I was in seventh grade, our student minister invited people to talk about what God was doing in our lives in a service where anyone could come in front of everyone to share. As usual, it took what seemed like forever before anyone got up the nerve to share with everyone. But eventually a girl named Cindy went to the front. I'll never forget what she said. She confidently took the microphone and said, "I'm Cindy, and God is showing me that I am holy. He's pleased with me. I love knowing who I am in Christ." It wasn't a long, drawn-out story—just a few words about her relationship with God. I don't know what shocked me more: that she only talked for ten seconds, or that she said she was holy. I remember thinking she was some sort of religious nut to say that. I whispered to a buddy beside me, "God is the only one who is holy, not us!" I mean, how in the world could she have the audacity to say that in front of people? But the truth was that Cindy knew the Bible and I did not. Had I been familiar with the word of God, I would have understood exactly what she was saying.

Read Colossians 1:15-23

Fill in the blanks:
Colossians 1:22 says, "But now he has reconciled you by Christ's physical body through death to present _____ _____ in his sight, without _____ and free from _____."

■ What do you think Paul meant when he wrote, "To present you holy in his sight"?

_____

_____

_____

_____

_____

■ What does it mean to be "without blemish and free from accusation"?

_____

_____

_____

■ How does this verse change the way we see ourselves?

_____

_____

_____

This truth is awesome! When God looks at me, he sees his son Jesus. The cleansing blood of Jesus Christ covers me. God is pleased with Jesus, and he is pleased with me. There is no more condemnation on my life (Romans 8:1).

If you are a Christian, then you are holy in God's sight. The problem for many of us as Christians is that we don't think this way. We let our minds dwell on so many things beside this concept. One way to get rooted in grace is to think on truths like this one. Meditating on God's word and thinking about yourself the way God does can and will change your view of yourself. Instead of seeing ourselves as pathetic sinners who have no worth, we need to focus and train our minds so we can see ourselves as God sees us.

prayer exercise:

Take a few moments and meditate upon the following truths about yourself. Even though these thoughts may seem foreign to you, they are from God's word. Train yourself to think on these things. Say the following prayer aloud: "Father, teach me to see myself the way you see me. Open my eyes to the reality of who I am in you. I want to be rooted in grace. I want to see myself the way you see me, loving Father. I love you. Help me learn today." Now, read aloud the following truths:

- God sees Jesus in me.
- I am identified with Jesus.
- Jesus has presented me before God as holy.
- I am pleasing to God.
- God likes me.
- Because of Jesus, there is no accusation against me from God.

licensed
to sin

There is nothing like being saturated in God's love. To know that the Creator of the world is full of love and wants to walk through life with us is an amazing concept. Many of our heroes from the Bible understood God's tender and loving heart, and that knowledge changed their lives. God's love for us changes things. It changes the way we see ourselves, our families, our friends, and even God himself. But underneath this truth, one question comes up over and over: "If God loves me so much and he sees Jesus in me, then does it matter what I do? Can I do anything I want?"

■ Do you think it matters what we do?
- ❏ yes
- ❏ no

Explain your answer.

_____

_____

_____

_____

■ If God loves you no matter what you do, what keeps you from fulfilling your desires in sinful ways?

_____

_____

_____

I'm not a big hunter, but I want to be like the guys I see on television who shoot the huge buck and go after the big bears. I'd like to go into the woods and be an outdoorsman of sorts. But I have to admit I'm not the sportsman I aspire to be. On the other hand, my brother-in-law is the most avid deer hunter I know. He loves it so much you could call it an obsession. When we're driving down the road, he'll often shout, "There goes a deer!" He's always looking for his next big buck. I've gone with him a couple of times to sit in his deer stand. It's a pretty neat feeling to be out in the middle of nowhere waiting for animals to come by.

When I started talking to my brother in law about what it means to be a hunter, the first thing he talked about was getting a license. To hunt deer legally, you need to have a valid hunting license issued annualy by the state in which you will be hunting. There are no two ways about it. And you can only hunt deer during the specific season designated by the state for deer hunting. Most states even require you to buy a special annual deer permit that is purchased in addtion to the cost of the general hunting license. I'm looking forward to getting my license and proper permits so I can hunt legally in my state. When I get my hunting license, I will in essence have **permission** to hunt.

But imagine this scenario: I get my hunting license and go into the woods with my brother-in-law. On the ride there, I say, "Man, I'm looking forward to bagging some people today." My brother-in-law would swerve off of the road and scream at me for saying such a thing. It's unthinkable. Just having a hunting license doesn't mean you can hunt whatever you want.

Read Romans 6

■ How does Paul react to the question we looked at earlier today?

_____

_____

_____

_____

■ How is Paul's reaction like my brother-in-law's in the hunting scenario?

_____

_____

_____

_____

_____

_____

■ Why doesn't God's grace give us a license to do whatever we want?

_____

_____

_____

_____

_____

_____

Paul is faced with this same question four different times in Romans. This book is Paul's masterpiece on God's grace, and after a while people started wondering whether grace gave them a license to do whatever they wanted. Paul's response was dramatic and emphatic. He exclaims, "By no means!" The truth that God loves us and has bestowed his grace upon us does not entitle us to do whatever we want. Like a package stamped "Handle with care," we have a great responsibility as we live in God's great grace.

Take some time to confess to God today.
Tell him that you never want to take
his love and grace for granted. Admit
to him how you have done that in the
past, and ask for his forgiveness.
Express to your Father how seriously
you take the responsibility of grace.
Tell him how much you want to please
him with your life. Open your heart to
the Lord and tell him how much you love
him and how thankful you are for grace.

transforming
grace

Read Jeremiah 18:1-6

■ Where and how can you trace the hand of God in your life?

_____

_____

_____

_____

■ Respond to this statement: God's grace is more than just information; it is about transformation.

_____

_____

_____

_____

Grace is a loaded concept. It's God's gift to mankind. We experience love and acceptance under grace. Grace gives us tremendous freedom. As we've seen all week, God's grace is truly amazing.

However, to talk about God's grace only in terms of being accepted sells short what grace really is. Grace is not just information about who I am in Christ and how God accepts me. It's so much more than that. Grace changes us. God is into transforming his people. As a potter molds the clay in his hand, God desires to mold us. When the clay collapses and the work is marred, God is persistent with grace, taking time to form us again into the vessel he intends us to be. We miss the message of grace if we keep it on an informational level. God has so much more in store for us than that.

■ Is God's grace transforming you on a daily basis?

☐ yes
☐ no

If so, how? If not, why not?

_____

_____

_____

_____

■ How do you know if God's grace is transforming you?

_____

_____

_____

■ What does it look like to live this way?

_____

_____

_____

_____

A friend who happens to be a co-worker of mine has a plant in his office. I see him watering it, tending to the leaves or making sure it is in appropriate sunlight almost every day. If there are any dead leaves on it, he will prune them to ensure it stays healthy. He cares for it like a mother cares for her baby. When I watch him taking care of this plant, I always notice how gentle he is with it. He does not have to announce to the entire office that he cares about the plant or that he wants it to do well. His actions demonstrate that.

I can't help but think about our Father when I see my friend with this plant. In much the same way, God loves to work with us and groom us into followers of him. He does this through his grace. His love transforms us below the surface in ways we can only see with eyes focused on spiritual things. When we renew our minds about the love of God, something happens. The picture Jeremiah gives in this passage is beautiful. God is the potter, and we are the clay. This picture exudes God's grace. We see grace in the way the potter's hands deal with the clay. Our God loves to transform us into beautiful pieces of art.

■ How does it make you feel to know that God desires to mold you in his grace?

❑ joyful   ❑ loved
❑ vulnerable   ❑ trusting
❑ peaceful   ❑ other _____

prayer exercise:

Read Jeremiah 18:1-6 again. As you read, focus on the interaction between the potter and the clay. Picture how gently a potter holds his clay. There is an experience there that is more than just acquiring or offering information.

This page is designed to give you space to take notes during your "Redefining Normal" group session or to journal your reflections on the highlights of this week's study.

REDEFINING NORMAL

MORAL BOUNDARIES

moving from "no" to "yes"

the crucified
life

■ Have you ever been in a car with someone who drove with reckless abandon?

❑ yes
❑ no

If so, describe that experience.

_____

_____

_____

_____

■ Have you ever been in a car with someone who refused to ask for directions?

❑ yes
❑ no

If so, describe that experience.

_____

_____

_____

_____

_____

_____

_____

There are two scenarios where I hate being in a car. The first is when the person driving the car has no regard for my life. Somehow, that person fails to realize that the machine he or she is operating has the potential to send us to our graves. Such out-of-control drivers carelessly weave in and out of traffic, violate all the rules of the road and leave you grasping the handle above the door with a death grip not even a wrestler like The Rock™ could break. If you finally reach your destination, you kiss the ground and promise never to get in a vehicle driven by this so-called friend again.

The second vehicle scenario that bugs me to no end occurs when I am riding with someone who refuses to stop and ask for directions. I can't always blame others for this trait; I myself commit this infraction from time to time, but I always know where I'm going. (Yeah, right.) Driving around for what feels like an eternity because of someone's pride can be frustrating. Going one hundred miles in the wrong direction has the potential to make someone turn violent. I'll never forget the scene from *Dumb and Dumber* when Lloyd drove through the night in the wrong direction. The rage Harry showed when he realized what Lloyd had done is a perfect picture of the way we all feel in this situation.

We look at these scenarios today because these two pictures perfectly illustrate the two traps into which Christians fall time and time again. One school of thought says that grace means we have been handed the keys to the car and can drive any way we choose. Who cares about the rules? There aren't any. We touched on this subject last week as we looked at whether grace is a license to sin. The other school of thought says that Christian living is all about the rules. As long as you obey the traffic rules, you are a good Christian. The truth is that both of these perspectives miss the point. Reckless drivers often forget that traffic rules are there for their own protection. These rules are not set up to keep them from experiencing joy as drivers but to insure they will be driving for a long time. On the other hand, drivers who are sticklers for every traffic law may forget that, while following the rules is important, it is not the end in itself. It's possible to follow all the rules and still end up in the wrong place. If I want to go from Florida to North Carolina, I must go north. If I go south on Interstate 95, I can follow all the rules and still never get to North Carolina.

- What did Peter say should never happen to Jesus?
  - ❑ He should never be mocked.
  - ❑ He should never be a success.
  - ❑ He should never die.

- How did Jesus answer Peter's objection?
  - ❑ by encouraging him
  - ❑ by thanking him
  - ❑ by rebuking him

Fill in the blanks:
Matthew 16:24 says, "Then Jesus said to his _____, 'If _____ would come after me, he must _____ himself and take up his _____ and follow me.'"

   In Matthew 16, Jesus shows us a different way of life. It is a road that seems strange, but it is one we all must travel. Jesus says that to follow him we will have to crucify ourselves. It seems ridiculous at first, so we object much like Peter did. Must following Jesus really go through the Cross? Jesus remains insistent. Life can only be found through both passion and crucifixion. This week we're going to talk about moral boundaries by looking at the passionate pursuit of God and the crucifixion of earthly things. To do this, we must first understand the truth that saying "Yes" to something means saying "No" to other things. Saying "No" is not the essence of Christian life, although the ability to say "No" to temptation and other hindrances does play a role in our walk with Christ. We say "No" to some things so that we can say "Yes" to the most important things. Christianity is not a set of rules without directions; neither is it saying "Yes" to everything.

■ Has being a Christian ever cost you anything?

❑ yes
❑ no

If so, what did it cost you? If not, why not?

_____

_____

_____

_____

As you think about this question, evaluate your life and spend some time in solitude listening for any direction from God. Use the space provided to journal your thoughts and God's response.

_____

_____

_____

_____

an enemy
lurks

I don't know about you, but it seems as though every time I really have a desire and hunger for the Lord, I meet opposition. Why is it that when people take the Lord seriously, they always seem to face more persecution? Not long ago, I prayed, "Lord, I want to make you the absolute Master of my life. I want to completely surrender everything to you." Within a few days, roadblocks to my walk with Christ were popping up everywhere. Temptations and distractions seemed to multiply after I prayed that prayer. My flesh reared its ugly head, and I had to battle sin at an increased level. It was obvious to me that there is an enemy in my life who would love nothing more than to keep me from surrendering everything in my life to Jesus.

■ Have you gone through a period in your life where you knew the enemy was trying to take you down?

❏ yes
❏ no

If so, explain that situation.

_____

_____

_____

_____

■ What gets in the way of your walk with Christ?

❏ sinful patterns   ❏ other people
❏ boredom   ❏ selfishness
❏ busyness   ❏ pride

■ Why does the enemy come against
  believers so much?

_____

_____

_____

_____

Read John 10:1-21

Fill in the blanks:
In John 10:10, Jesus says: "The _____
comes _____ to _____ and _____;
I have come that they may have _____,
and have it to the _____."

Kerry decided that it was time for her to take her relationship with Jesus more seriously. She was sick and tired of riding the fence. She loved Jesus and knew that he had saved her from her sins, but she wanted to grow. On a retreat, Kerry made the decision that she wanted to live as God intended. She became very emotional as she realized how much God loved her. She was ready to conquer the world for Christ when she headed back to school and her normal routine of life the following Monday.

But a funny thing happened when she went back to school. Kerry found herself being tempted in ways she had never experienced—to say unkind things about her friends, to lie to her teachers and to do things she knew were wrong. On top of this, she was constantly fighting with her parents. Suddenly, she felt a million miles away from God. Kerry didn't know what was happening. Her emotions were a wreck, her family life was struggling, her friends were putting a lot of pressure on her and she couldn't figure anything out.

Kerry was so thrown by the whole experience that she went to one of the leaders of her youth group and asked for advice. The leader shared with her about how the enemy will do anything he can to interfere with a believer's walk with Jesus. That's when Kerry remembered the commitment to the

Lord she had made on the retreat. Suddenly, she realized how real it was to be attacked by the enemy.

■ **Jesus says that he comes to give us life to the full. What do you think this promise means?**

_____

_____

_____

Thank God that Jesus has an answer to the attacks of our enemy. Sin is very real, and it is a force that wants to take us down. There is no doubt that Satan hates for people to follow Jesus. As we talk about moral boundaries, it helps to remember the truth about the lurking enemy. All of us have been or will be in situations like Kerry's. We all struggle in our Christian walk because Satan wants to devour us. He wants us to live second-rate lives, and he lies to us and lures us in an attempt to pull away from the life God intends for us. He even makes misery pleasurable for a short time, only to leave us worse off in the end. God, on the other hand, wants to give us life to the full. God is the one who has our best interests at heart. Moving from saying "No" to saying "Yes" means choosing God's way over the enemy's even in times of great persecution. This is the path to freedom.

prayer exercise:

Read Ephesians 6:10-18 out loud and make it your prayer for today. Discuss with God how you want to stand strong in his might, no matter what the enemy brings your way. Ask him to arm you to withstand the enemy.

stripping down
and suiting up

Warning labels seem to be on everything nowadays. With all the frivolous lawsuits that have made their way through our court system, companies now think they must warn us about everything to protect themselves from liability. Below are some outrageous disclaimers we obtained from a popular Web site.[1] Who knows if these warnings are really used by companies, but you get the point.

- Name-brand hairdryer: "Do not use while sleeping."
- Container of bread pudding: "Product will be hot after heating."
- Clothing iron box: "Do not iron clothes on body."
- Sleep aid bottle: "Warning: may cause drowsiness"
- Chainsaw: "Do not attempt to stop chain with your hand."
- Super-Hero costume: "Wearing of this garment does not enable you to fly."

With examples like these, it's no wonder we fail to take warnings seriously. A few months ago, I was leaving my office to go home for the day when I heard warning sirens signaling that a severe storm was in the area. Of course, I did what most people do—I ignored the warning. I thought, *I live in South Carolina. These people are absolutely ridiculous. They don't know what a severe storm is. They sound the sirens every time they see a flash of lightning. I don't need to listen to them. Now, if I lived in Oklahoma or Kansas, it would be different.*

But when I got about halfway home, I began to wonder about my decision. The wind was gusting opposite ways on either side of the street, the sky had a greenish tint that I had only seen before on TLC's *Storm Stories* and a TV crew was waiting to talk to a guy in a white tank-top standing outside his mobile home. That's when I figured out that I was in trouble. I turned my car around at breakneck speed, sped back to my office, ran into the building and hid under a desk. It's only when you come into contact with the something as real as a storm that you understand why we should take warnings seriously. God warns us because he loves us.

■ What things does Paul say to put off in this passage?

_____

_____

_____

_____

■ What things does Paul say to put on in this passage?

_____

_____

_____

_____

Colossians 3:1-17 is our theme passage for the week. In it, Paul cautioned the believers at Colosse—people he had called holy just a few chapters earlier—to avoid some behaviors and pursue others. His summed up the "stripping down" process in the following way: "Set your minds on things above, not on earthly things" (verse 2). Paul is saying here that something wonderful happens in our lives at salvation. God resurrects who we really are. Brokenness no longer has control over us, and our lives become destined for blessing. But in order to embrace the person we become at salvation, there needs to be some stripping away of the old person so that the new person can come forth.

If you have ever been sunburned to the point of peeling, you can understand the illustration. New skin has arrived, but the old skin must be peeled away so that the new skin can breathe. In a similar way, although we are transformed at the moment of salvation, the rest of our lives will be spent recognizing the new and stripping away the old.

■ What are some things you struggle with as part of your old nature? (Check all that apply.)

☐ sexual sin ☐ pride ☐ anger
☐ lust ☐ greed ☐ gossip
☐ bitterness ☐ hatred ☐ words

■ Do you ever find yourself getting as close to "the line" with these sins as you can?

☐ yes
☐ no

It is sad how many times we as Christians try to live as people of the world. God calls us to be separate. While God does not intend for us to isolate ourselves from the world, he wants us to know that we are not supposed to be of the world. While the old person begs us to live as close to "the line" as possible, this passage encourages us to seek better behaviors. Instead of sexual sin, God invites us to pursue purity. Instead of anger, he invites us to pursue kindness. Instead of gossip, he invites us to pursue encouragement.

God warns us about the old person and encourages us toward the new person not because he is trying to micromanage our lives but because he knows how dangerous lust, sexual sin, anger, greed, gossip and the rest of these sins are. He warns us because he loves us.

■ What do you need to say "No" to in your life?

_____

_____

_____

_____

_____

Spend some time today repenting for those things God's Spirit has identified as sin in your life. Remember that repenting means not only saying you are sorry but also turning away from your sins as well. This may mean spending some time in struggle as you ask God to change your desires. Let that struggle define your prayer time today.

notes

1. "Funny Warning Labels," (http://members.aol.com/weirdnessm/Page31.html)

flirting
with disaster

Have you ever noticed that it's not until you have a boyfriend or girlfriend that your dating possibilities suddenly seem endless? You could literally go for years without dating someone, having the word "available" all but tattooed across your forehead, desperate for a relationship but finding no one. Finally, someone special comes across your path, and you start dating. Then out of nowhere three or four more attractive, intriguing people start showing interest in you. Why is this? I think it comes down to one truth: we are magnetically attracted to things we can't have.

Most of the time, when you find yourself in a situation like this, you are left with a few options. You could break up with the person you're dating and try to date someone else. This rarely works out well, because it's not attractive to be willing to break off a relationship so casually, and once you're available again, you lose your unavailable lure. Another option is to sneak around and date other people. Quite often this option produces undesirable consequences, because it's hard to build trust in a relationship that started only because trust was broken elsewhere. The third option is to make the most of the relationship you're a part of, realizing that your perception and reality are often very different things. While this usually is the best decision, it is not always the one we make.

Or you could do what many people choose to do: stay in the relationship but flirt with other people. In our minds, this gives us the best of both worlds. We get to stay in a relationship but still get the intrigue of building a "relationship" with others, even if it is just in our minds. And since we haven't necessarily crossed the line to cheating on our companions, we convince ourselves there's no harm in playing flirtatious head games with others. Rarely do our significant others see our playing both fields as innocent behavior—the women on the hit reality TV show, *The Bachelor,* have trouble with this even though they sign up for it. But we convince ourselves we could be doing far worse things, so flirting must be innocent fun.

Today's devotion is not about dating etiquette. You can work that issue out on your own. Instead, we're looking at a much broader issue, our tendency to flirt with sin. Inside all of us is a pull toward things we know we shouldn't do. And while we may be scared to cross the line and cheat, many times we choose to flirt. We get as close to the line as we can without crossing it. The story of Samson gives us a great look at this tendency.

Read Judges 13-14

■ What was the specific call on Samson's life?
- ☐ to be a king
- ☐ to be a Nazirite
- ☐ to be a prophet
- ☐ to be a priest

■ Being a _____ meant that Samson was to avoid certain behaviors. Mark the behaviors that Samson was to avoid as required by his vow. (Numbers 6 has a list that can help.) Check all that apply.

- ☐ cutting his hair
- ☐ drinking anything from a vine
- ☐ eating shellfish
- ☐ drinking goat's milk
- ☐ touching dead animals
- ☐ getting married

■ What two vows does Samson break by the end of chapter 14?

_____

_____

_____

_____

Samson gives us a great picture of Israel's journey throughout the book of Judges, and it's a picture of our lives as well. Israel was playing a game of spiritual ping-pong, bouncing back and forth between seeking God and seeking the things God hates. Within each of us is a great potential for good and a great potential for evil. While most of the time we don't intentionally seek to do outright evil, we flirt with things that are less than God's best for us, and before we know it we fall flat on our face. Before we fall, we usually flirt.

This was the case with Samson. Because he was distinguished as a Nazirite, he was not to drink the fruit of the vine, but we see him walking through a vineyard. We see a man who was not supposed to touch dead animals "turning aside" to look at the lion he had killed (14:8). And by the end of chapter 14, he had broken two of his three vows; cutting his hair was the only one he had not violated. We can't say for sure that Samson fell into sin only because he made poor decisions and flirted with sin, but the story suggests that's what happened in his case.

■ Do you ever find yourself tempted to flirt with the things of this world?

❑ yes
❑ no

■ Have you ever fallen because you flirted with sin?

❑ yes
❑ no

If so, what steps did you take in your life to reverse the pattern?

_____

_____

_____

_____

_____

We must be clear about what God is saying. Samson did not violate his covenant with God by walking through the vineyard. He didn't violate his covenant by looking at the lion he had killed. He simply underestimated his own weakness. Instead of protecting his vow, he let his guard down. Before he knew it, he had compromised on the things that were most important to him. We too must be careful to not let our guards down. Our enemy is a roaring lion who wants to devour us. While we don't want to drift into legalism by making inflexible rules for areas which God doesn't set concrete standards, we must always be honest with ourselves about our own weaknesses and develop personal convictions that help us focus on God. When we focus on God, he will help us overcome our tendency to get sidetracked from his best in our lives.

prayer exercise:

Think back today over some of the times that you have fallen into sin in the past. Did flirting with the sin play any role in your fall? In what areas in your life are you the weakest spiritually? Take some time today to ask God if there are any convictions he would want to form in you to help you in those areas of weakness.

bread and
narrow gates

Read Matthew 7:13-14

■ What do you think Jesus means by the narrow gate?

_____

_____

_____

_____

■ How do you enter the narrow gate instead of the wide gate?

_____

_____

_____

_____

■ Why do you think it is harder to enter through the narrow gate than the wide gate?

_____

_____

_____

_____

Max was a typical 4-year-old. He loved to play and run around his house. Like many preschoolers, he was a little on the hyperactive side and had a hard time listening to his parents when they told him to do something. Max's parents told him about things he was not supposed to touch, such as the knives in the kitchen drawer and the gasoline in his dad's shed. But Max liked to do his own thing; he didn't like being told what to do. One day, as he was exploring under the kitchen sink, he came upon some cleaning supplies. His mother saw him and said, "Max, put that down. It's too dangerous for you." But Max was having fun, so he picked up the bottle and drank the liquid in it. When he did, his mother screamed. Max started to feel sick right away, and his mom grabbed him, put him in the car and headed to the hospital. The doctors pumped Max's stomach and kept him for observation overnight.

This episode gave Max a big life lesson about listening to his parents. He figured out that when his parents told him to stay away from something dangerous, he should, because they knew what they were talking about.

■ Do you sometimes take the things Jesus said too lightly?

❑ yes
❑ no

If so, why do you take Jesus' teaching lightly? How do you take it lightly?

_____

_____

_____

_____

In today's passage, Jesus said something pretty dramatic. He says that many people enter through the wide gate, which is the gate to destruction, and only a small number of people enter through the narrow gate. This statement is quite alarming! However, I fear that most people don't take this statement or any of the other statements Jesus made seriously enough. We're like Max heading to the cabinet with the cleaning supplies.

But Jesus calls us to enter the narrow gate and to live by his instructions so that we may journey on the road to life. Only few choose to enter this gate and thus find life.

Most people really believe that the Christian commandments (for example, to love one's neighbor as oneself) are intentionally a little too severe—like putting the clock ahead half an hour to make sure of not being late in the morning.[1]

It's very popular today to think that God does absolutely everything. It is true that he is sovereign and powerful and committed to working out his re-creative plan on earth. But there is one thing that he has never done and will never do: force people to choose the narrow gate. If someone sits back and waits on God to push him through the narrow gate, he will be waiting his entire life. God has presented us with truth, but the choice is up to us. It's not enough to say "No" to the wide gate. We must say "Yes" to the life of the narrow gate and walk through it.

Entering the narrow gate means simply surrendering your life to Jesus every single day. It's saying "Yes" to Jesus. The life of surrender says "Yes" to Jesus as master. We've described that process this week as crucifying the desires of the flesh and passionately pursuing the life God intends us to have. Redefining normal means more than saying "No" to the wide gate. It means walking through the narrow one.

■ Are you living a life of surrender?
❑ yes
❑ no

If not, what can you do to walk the "straight and narrow" today?

_____

_____

_____

Express to God your desire to live a life of surrender, a life that goes through the narrow gate. If there is anything in your life you need to confess to your Father, do it now. Tell him how seriously you take his words and commands. Spend a few moments reflecting and asking him to show you what it means to live a life of surrender.

notes:

1. Soren Kierkegaard. W. H. Auden and Louis Kronenberger, eds., *The Viking Book of Aphorisms* (New York: Barnes and Noble, 1993), 80.

_____

_____

_____

_____

_____

_____

_____

_____

_____

_____

_____

_____

_____

    This page is designed to give you space to take notes during your "Redefining Normal" group session or to journal your reflections on the highlights of this week's study.

REDEFINING NORMAL

SPIRITUAL DISCIPLINES

for us, not for God

an atmosphere
for growth

Read Mark 4:1-20

■ List the four kinds of soil described by Jesus in these verses and what happened to the seed planted in each kind of soil.

_____

_____

_____

_____

_____

_____

■ Write out the message of this parable in your own words in ten words or less.

_____

_____

_____

In this parable, the same types of seed fall on four different types of soil. In the story, the type of soil determines which seeds would be productive. The first three kinds of soil do not allow the seed to grow and flourish, but the good soil produces a surprisingly abundant crop.

So far on our journey of *Redefining Normal*, we have challenged the norm, grappled with grace, and discussed a different approach to moral boundaries. This week we continue the journey by talking about how spiritual disciplines are for us, not for God. Just as a seed needs good soil to grow, we need the atmosphere these disciplines provide to grow spiritually. Spiritual disciplines are not the marks of a good Christian; they help to create the atmosphere that forms us into people of faith, hope, and love.

Patience and perseverance are difficult words for most of us. We like things on our terms, and we like growth to be quick. This is never more evident than in the way we often study for tests. Actually, study is not the right word; the truth is that we cram. I have a friend—we'll call him George—who basically tried to learn the whole Hebrew language in one night. It was not that he didn't want to know Hebrew before then, but all semester, he kept delaying the inevitable. Before he knew it, it was the night before the final exam, and to his horror he realized he had a long way to go if he was going to pass. It's not that he didn't attend class. He did. It's not that he didn't do his homework. He completed most of his assignments on time. But throughout the year, he found other things to fill his time that were just a little more pressing. He completed the assignments but didn't learn the material. So he embarked on a one-night cram session to learn the Hebrew language.

I'd like to report that things went well for George on the final exam. The truth is they didn't. He woke up the morning of the exam with a frightening thought: "I don't know anything!" As we drove to school, a friend and I sat in the front seats and quizzed each other back and forth. George sat in the back, face against the window, drool coming out of his mouth, with the most helpless and hopeless look on his face. Things didn't get any better once the test started. You know you're in bad shape when you start adding up your highest possible score midway through the exam and the best you can do is a 42. Let's just say that George had seen better days.

Sadly, cramming also defines many of our relationships with God. We don't really care about knowing God until we get in a crunch. When we are in a crunch, we read, pray, and seek God in any way possible. We hope that somehow reading and praying and seeking will help us through the crisis. The trouble is that we never really get to know God in the process, because we're just looking for a way out.

■ How does Paul say that transformation will occur in our lives?

❏ by doing whatever we want
❏ by cramming
❏ by renewing our minds

■ Complete this sentence: Renewing
your mind is a _____.

❏ once-a-year thing
❏ once-a-week thing
❏ continual thing

There is no cut-and-dried way to create good soil in our lives. Renewing
the mind will look somewhat different for each of us. But over the years,
many saints have found things such as reading the Bible, prayer, solitude,
meditation, service, corporate worship, and music helpful. Modern writers
have termed these things **spiritual disciplines**. These disciplines
were never intended to be ends in and of themselves, much less the meas-
urement of what a good Christian looks like. But they are ingredients that
help create the atmosphere in which much of our spiritual growth takes
place. We do not read the Bible or pray because this is what good Christians
do. We read the Bible, pray, and use the other disciplines to slow us down so
that we can know God not in a cram session but in a relationship. As we
learn more and more about who he is, our attitudes and behaviors will
change. By cultivating the soil of our lives, we not only sin less; we embrace
the things God values most—faith, hope, and love. We slowly become the
people God intends us to be and live the lives he intends us to live. This week
we will be looking at a few disciplines that help create an atmosphere for
growth in our lives.

Evaluate the ways you have used the spiritual disciplines in the past. Have they functioned more as a checklist or as an atmosphere for spiritual growth? Have they been a part of your life at all? Ask God to teach what it means for you individually to be good soil for his word. Ask him what activities and disciplines he wants to become regular parts of your life. Commit to spend this week experimenting with some spiritual disciplines.

scripture
discipline #1

I love food. One of my best friends is somewhat of a gourmet cook, and I love watching him fix dishes I can't even pronounce. He takes all sorts of flavorings and spices and blends them together with whatever he is making, and out pops a delicious meal. I get so excited when he says, "Hey man, taste this and tell me what you think."

One day I was thinking about why I loved to eat the food he prepares, and I figured it out. It's not deep philosophical reason that will move you to tears, but the reason I love his cooking so much is that he knows how to make it taste good. Taste is one of God's gifts to us. Think about all the different kinds of foods we enjoy—Mexican, Italian, Chinese, Thai, and more. Concentrating on what these foods taste like is enough to make you start drooling. I don't know about you, but I'm suddenly hungry.

Read Psalm 34:8

Fill in the blanks:
Psalm 34:8a says, "_____ and see that the _____ is _____."

■ What does it mean to taste and see the Lord's goodness?

_____

_____

_____

_____

I'm in my 30s now, and I'm pretty bummed. I'm bummed that it has taken me this long to see how wonderful it is to be in God's word. I feel as though I wasted so many years when I could have been enjoying God's goodness. Don't get me wrong; I have always respected God's word. I've always known that it is real and that it contains power. The problem was that I hardly ever picked up the Bible and started tasting. One of the greatest ways we can taste and see that the Lord is good is through his written word.

Imagine that you drove to a swanky steakhouse to eat a great meal, but once you pulled in the parking lot, you never went inside. What good does a steakhouse do for you if you never go in and taste the food? We have to pick up God's word and taste it. Reading, studying, and saturating ourselves in God's word leads to life. It tastes better than anything in the world.

■ **Do you spend time experiencing God's goodness through his word?**

❏ yes
❏ no

If so, how do you do that? If not, why not?

_____

_____

_____

■ **How do you feel about reading and studying Scripture?**

❏ I enjoy it.
❏ I don't enjoy it because I don't understand it.
❏ I dread it.
❏ I do it because I'm supposed to.
❏ I do it when I have time.
❏ I learn something almost every time I do.

Most of the students with whom I cross paths feel that reading the Bible is kind of a hassle. But every once in a while, I encounter someone who always seems to want to spend more time in the word. Have you ever wondered what the difference between these two kinds of people is? I believe that the person who enjoys studying Scripture will know that God loves him or her and that this written record of God's words is meant to bring life. God never intended for the Bible to be something people hated to read. God's intention is for you to taste and to see how awesome he is through his word. Most of the things I read about spiritual disciplines when it comes to Scripture usually make me feel guilty about not reading the Bible more often. But I think God looks at things differently than I do. Redefining normal when it comes to Scripture reading is learning about who God is, who I am, what God values, and what I should value. The story of beauty, brokenness, baptism, and blessing is the story of the Bible, and if we are going to embrace this life of blessing, we must read the Bible and see how our spiritual forefathers have done so.

God is not going to love you any more just because you increase your time spent in his word. However, you will start loving him more. You will see who he truly is. You will start tasting how good he is, and you won't want to put his word down.

prayer exercise:

Begin by praying this prayer: "Father, I want to taste and see that you are good through your scripture today. Open my eyes as I read from your word, and teach me about it. I love you." Then look up the following verses.

- Deuteronomy 8:3
- Psalm 119:105
- Hebrews 4:12
- 2 Timothy 3:16

Read these verses slowly several times. Pray about the things they teach you about scripture. Let God reveal the truth about his word as you do. After you have done this, pray and praise God for his word.

prayer
discipline #2

Prayer is a fascinating thing when you think about it. It blows my mind to think that right now, wherever we are, you and I can talk to the Creator of the world, and he will hear us. I don't know about you, but that excites me to no end. God is teaching me so much about prayer and how powerful it is. I have gone from not knowing a lot about prayer and its purpose to enjoying and looking forward to talking with God.

■ How do you feel about prayer?
- ❑ I look forward to praying each day.
- ❑ I can't pray without falling asleep.
- ❑ I feel guilty about how little I pray.
- ❑ I want to pray, but I'm always too distracted.
- ❑ I feel like my prayers are just words hitting the ceiling.
- ❑ Other _____

■ How often do you pray?
- ❑ once a day or more
- ❑ once every few days
- ❑ once a week
- ❑ once a month
- ❑ never

■ What does your prayer time look like?

_____

_____

_____

■ How do you think God thinks about prayer? What is he looking for in our prayer lives?

_____

_____

_____

One of my best friends is the other author of this book. His name is Dave, and if you want to see what he looks like, his picture is on the back cover of this book. (He'll hate the fact that I am writing about him, but he'll get over it.) In 1996, God called us into ministry together, and ever since then, we have been learning and walking with God together. The thing I love about Dave is that I can sit down with him any time and have great conversations about God, life, and people. Do you have a friend with whom you can talk about anything, and even if you disagree on something, work it out and learn in the process? That's how my friendship with Dave is. We can talk about anything.

Even though I love these things about our friendship, the things I like most are the times where we just hang out and watch football. We may go an hour without even saying a word to each other. In those times, we're not trying to solve the world's problems or discuss deep theological truths. We're sitting in the same room and hanging out. I think that's what true friends are, people with whom you can hang out and enjoy their presence.

■ What do your prayers usually sound like? Do they consist mainly of things you are asking God for, or struggles you are dealing with, or other things?

_____

_____

_____

_____

In this chapter, Adam and Eve had just eaten the forbidden fruit. But we're not going to focus on that sinful act today. Instead, notice something many people never see: verse 8 tells us that God "was walking in the garden in the cool of the day."

Have you ever thought about what it must have been like for Adam and Eve in that garden before they sinned? Think about it for a second: these two human beings were in the garden enjoying not just everything that God had made; they were enjoying God himself. God would walk and talk with Adam and Eve. It fascinates me to think about the kind of relationship they had with God. What do you think that they talked about? I can guarantee you that until this point they had no sin to confess, no suffering people for whom to intercede, no inner turmoil to overcome, no bad thoughts to cast away. I can just imagine some of their conversations with God. Eve would say to God, "I was noticing some flowers today, and I just want to tell you that they are beautiful." Maybe God would respond, "Thanks, Eve, they're some of my favorites also. Aren't they awesome?" They must have had some unbelievable times hanging out with each other.

■ Do you ever spend time like this talking with God about how awesome he is and how much you love him without asking him for anything?

☐ yes
☐ no

Why or why not?

_____

_____

_____

My fear is that most of us go to God only with our problems. Taking our problems to God is not wrong, but often we fail to take advantage of the opportunity to just hang out with our Father. God desires to talk with us and show us who he is, and he has provided prayer as a way for us to communicate with him. Our times of prayer with our God should consist mostly of being with him and sharing with him what we think of him. We should thank him for what his word says he thinks about us. Maybe, just maybe, we can even say, "Hello Father," and then sit in his presence without saying anything.

prayer exercise:

Use this time of prayer to do what we have been talking about during this devotion. Walk and talk with him in the cool of your day. Today, more than learning about prayer, we want to experience prayer. Take your time with this exercise, which is designed to help you get started.

P: Prepare—Calm your heart. Tell God why you love him and enjoy spending time with him.

R: Relax—Spend time in the cool of the day with God. There's no agenda here; just time to hang out. Talk to him and listen to him.

A: Ask—Take your needs to God. Tell him about your frustrations and struggles.

Y: Yearn—Ask God to create a desire in you for who he is and for his things. Take some time to let this desire start to grow.

E: Express—Tell God what you think about him. Show your love, adoration, and praise for him.

R: Remember—Think back to the ways God has led you in the past. Thank him for leading you to where you are today. Ask him to continue to guide you in the future as he has in the past.

meditation
discipline #3

Joshua
1:1-8

Meditation is a word that is misunderstood in Christian circles today. It sounds a little like New Age philosophy, but that is only because we don't understand what the word really means. If we did, we would be thrilled about practicing this discipline. God loves for us to meditate on him and his things. Today, we're going to talk about what meditation really is.

Read Joshua 1:1-8

Fill in the blanks:
Joshua 1:8 says, "Do not let this Book of the Law depart from your mouth; _____ on it _____ and _____, so that you may be careful to _____ _____ written in it. Then you will be _____ and _____."

This setting of this verse portrays a momentous time in the history of Israel. During this time, Joshua was taking the reigns of leadership from Moses, a follower of God who served the Lord and his people very well. Moses had led the Israelites out of Egypt all the way to the edge of the Promised Land. But now Moses was dead. It was now Joshua's turn to take over and lead God's people into the land the Lord had designated for them. Joshua was afraid and perhaps uncertain of his leadership skills. He was full of fear and apprehension about how he could take the place of a dynamic leader like Moses. Verse 8 describes God giving Joshua one of the keys to success. He tells him to meditate on God's law. That is a pretty important instruction. Joshua had a monumental task on his hands, and God said in so many words, "If you want to be successful, meditate on my word day and night, night and day."

■ What do you think it means to meditate on the words of God?

_____

_____

_____

My grandmother lives in a part of Georgia where there are a lot of farms. On our trips to see her when I was growing up, I remember seeing cows everywhere as we got near her house. Cows fascinated me when I was a kid. I don't know why. They don't run, they move really slowly, they make funny sounds, they smell bad, and they look weird. One of the things I noticed about cows when I was a child was that the cows always seemed to be eating and chewing grass. My grandmother would tell me, "Look, those cows are chewing the cud." I wondered for years what that meant. What is cud? It sounded a little disgusting.

As I grew older, I heard someone explain how a cow eats. I learned that a cow starts chewing on some grass and then it swallows it. Later, that grass will come back up from the cow's stomach so it can be chewed some more. The cow then swallows the cud into another stomach. Basically, a cow chews the grass, digests it, spits it up, chews on it some more, and then digests it again.

As I think about this picture of chewing the cud, I get a picture of what God was telling Joshua to do. He was instructing Joshua to chew the cud of his word. To meditate on God's word is to chew it, swallow it, digest it, bring it back up, chew it some more, and swallow again. The Hebrew word that is translated "meditate" in Joshua 1:8 is _hāgāh_, which means to speak or mutter the word over and over and never let it depart from your lips. That is the key to meditation—to mutter, or speak, and chew the cud with God's word.

■ Based on what you have learned today, what does it look like to take a passage of scripture and meditate on it?

_____

_____

Take Galatians 2:20 and meditate on it by doing the following:

- Mutter it by reading it aloud very slowly.

- Think about what you have just read.

- Read it aloud again.

- Write the verse down on a sheet of paper.

- Think about it some more.

- Try to recite it from memory.

- Talk to the Lord about what you see in it.

solitude
and silence

Matthew 14:13-33

Randy is the kind of guy who loves fellowship. He has more friends than he knows what to do with, and everyone loves being around him. He makes everyone laugh and is kindhearted to whomever he is around. Randy can always be seen with one or two of his friends. Whether he's driving down the road, at the mall, at a ballgame, watching a movie, or just hanging out, Randy never seems to be alone.

One day at church, Randy heard a guest speaker talking about solitude. He had no idea what in the world that word meant. He had never even heard this word before at church. As the speaker talked about the importance of spending time alone with God in silence, Randy felt a little uneasy, because he hated being by himself. He couldn't stand to be alone. But the speaker continued to talk about the benefits of connecting with God in silence and telling stories of how doing so had changed his relationship with the Father. Randy didn't know what to think as he listened and thought about what he was hearing.

■ **Have you ever spent an extended amount of time in silence with God?**

❑ yes

❑ no

If so, what was that time like? If not, what has kept you from doing this?

_____

_____

_____

_____

Randy decided to spend two hours alone in complete silence. For a person who was always around people, this was a big risk. He found a quiet place out in the middle of a huge field and put a blanket down to sit on. There he sat, just Randy, a blanket and a lot of silence. He really didn't know what to say to God. The only thing he could think to pray was, "Lord, here I am. I know you are here. Help me experience you as I spend some time with you in silence."

A funny thing happened over the next two hours. Randy actually enjoyed it! He never heard God say anything to him; nothing miraculous happened; and he never got goose bumps. But he did find it easier to focus on God in that setting. He felt like his time with God was valuable, even though his mind still wandered from time to time. The silence helped him focus as he shared his heart with God.

■ **Why do you think that the Lord wants us to spend time in silence with him?**

_____

_____

_____

■ **What are the benefits of silence?**

_____

_____

_____

Read Matthew 14:13-33

■ **Why do you think Jesus spent time in solitude and silence with God?**

_____

_____

_____

We live in a fast-paced society. It seems as though everything around us moves at the speed of light. A couple of months ago, I was in Orlando, Florida, and I felt so over-stimulated as I drove down International Drive. There were thousands of things going on around me. Buildings and billboards were lit up. People were everywhere enjoying all the tourist hot spots.

We're bombarded with noise and sights wherever we go. Turn on any cable news network, and you quickly learn you don't get one piece of news at a time—there are four things happening on the screen at once. There is a "talking head" delivering a news story, a stock-market ticker, the weather, and sports scores all at once. It's just way too much information to digest at one time. If we are not careful, we will let this flood of information and noise dominate our lives. We are busy people involved in so many things.

Jesus was busy too. He had many important things to do. Yet he always found time to be with God. He knew he needed time in solitude. And if Jesus, who was God's son, needed solitude, how much more do we need that time. Extended times of silence put us in position to focus on the Lord.

■ **How do you think times of solitude and silence would affect your walk with God? Would they help you on your journey? How so?**

_____

_____

_____

_____

_____

_____

solitude exercise:

Take some time to practice what we have learned about today. If you can, go for a walk somewhere it is really quiet. Find a place where you cannot and will not be disrupted for a while. Immerse yourself in the quiet and let God help you focus on him.

_____

_____

_____

_____

_____

_____

_____

_____

_____

_____

_____

_____

_____

_____

This page is designed to give you space to take notes during your "Redefining Normal" group session or to journal your reflections on the highlights of this week's study.

REDEFINING NORMAL

CONFESSION

when we mess up

heroes, legends
and normal guys

A couple years ago, I made a huge mistake. My wife had assigned me the husbandly duty of taking out the trash, a job I had done numerous times before. Time after time, I had completed this task without error. But this time, I only got it half-right. Taking out the trash was a little different for us during that period because we lived in the country, and there was no trash service available at the duplex we were renting. This meant that taking out the trash meant not only taking it out of the house but stopping by the local dumpster to dispose of it. I did the first part well. The second part, I did . . . not so well. I put the trash in the trunk of my car to drop off on the way to work. But with so many things on my mind and so much work to be done at the office, I simply forgot to drop the trash off in the dumpster.

The first day, my mistake wasn't even noticeable. But time began to pass, and since I rarely put things in the trunk of my car, the job remained half-done. I only began to realize something was wrong when I noticed a foul odor every time I drove my car. I was convinced that my wife had left some food in the car or spilled something in the back seat, so I searched ruthlessly there for the source of the smell. Of course, I found nothing. I blamed my air conditioning vents and even looked in my engine to see if an animal had crawled up and died there, but still no luck. Before long, I was driving everywhere with my windows down in an effort to avoid the odor, which was getting to be unbearable. Finally, my wife again asked me to take out the trash. I agreed to do my husbandly duty, and when I opened the trunk of my car to put the trash in, I found the garbage I had taken out several days before still sitting there. The stench was so bad when I popped the trunk that I almost passed out.

> Read 1 John 1:5-2:2

Fill in the blanks:
First John 1:8-9 says, "If we claim to be without _____, we _____ ourselves and the _____ is not in

us. If we _____ our _____, he
is _____ and _____ and will
_____ us our _____ and _____
us from all _____."

■ **How do you think most Christians
deal with sin in their lives?**

☐ cover it up   ☐ admit it
☐ hide it   ☐ ignore it
☐ blame someone else
☐ other _____

In this Scripture, John describes an interesting dilemma. He states in verses 5–6 that if we claim to have fellowship with God, who is light, but continue to walk in darkness, then we are liars. And then in verse 8, John says that if we claim to be without sin we deceive ourselves. This is the dilemma we all live in as Christians. Although we are walking the path of light on the whole, we still struggle with moments of darkness and sin in our lives. Although we rarely like to admit it, this is the truth about our lives. This week we must ask the question, "What happens when I mess up?"

Over the past four weeks, we have been on the adventure of redefining normal in our lives. We seek to grow in our relationship with God, and we long to say "Yes" to life as God intends it. But what are we to do in those moments when we temporarily choose another way, when we blow it, when we forget who we are and who God is? What happens when we sin?

We respond in a few different ways. Often we are convinced we are the only ones struggling with a particular sin, and so we hide ourselves, cover our sin or try to ignore its debilitating hold on our lives. Like Adam and Eve in the Garden, we too find ourselves in the shadows, putting up a brave face but afraid to show God the reality of our lives. But the truth of the Bible is that God is not shocked by our sin. On the contrary, he has dealt with the reality of our sin through the death of his son Jesus.

Time after time in the Bible, those who many of us would consider heroes and legends of the faith stumble in their walk with God. Yet we see in each of their stories that these people of God were not identified by their stumbles but by God's grace. It's not that God was pleased they stumbled. It's that he was sufficient in the middle of their stumbling.

Confession is the Christian response to sin in our lives. Confession is the way we take the trash out—not just out of sight, but to the dumpster to dispose of it. It is a tragedy of great proportions that so many of us have gotten so used to the smell of sin in our lives that we miss this radical opportunity to live in freedom under the aroma of grace.

Confession is simply being honest with God and those around us. It is admitting the times that we have messed up, turning away from the sins we have done and claiming the faithfulness of Christ in our lives. Through confession, we understand that when we sin our identity doesn't change—we are still saints, not sinners. We also remember that Christ has already paid our debt for our sin. We are hidden in him. Confession is not removing sin from God's view of us; it is owning up to our stumbles and coming back to Jesus, the source of forgiveness. He is faithful when we are unfaithful. He is just when we are unjust. In confession, even our sin becomes a catalyst for bringing us back to the cross. This week we will look in more detail at this vital aspect of embracing the life that God intends for us. We will seek to be honest about our humanity, but we will not settle for anything less than clinging to the cross in our lives.

prayer exercise:

Is there any sin that has left you in shadows, that you are struggling to cover up or that you have ignored in your life? What would it be like to step out of the shadows and into God's love? Are you willing to embrace Christ today by bringing him your trash? No sin is too big for him to handle. No hold is so tight that he cannot set you free. Today is the day to begin the journey of honesty and authenticity in our walks with Christ. Confess to him today.

a saint
who sins

■ Who are you? When you look at yourself, what do you see?

☐ failure   ☐ apathy
☐ greatness   ☐ holiness
☐ sin
☐ other _____

Explain your answer.

_____

_____

_____

What I am about to share with you is going to catch you off guard. Go to today's passage to find this revolutionary truth.

Read Ephesians 1:1

Fill in the blank:
Ephesians 1:1 says, "Paul, an apostle
of Christ Jesus by the will of God, to
the _____ in Ephesus, the
faithful in Christ Jesus."

■ Meditate on this verse for a few
minutes. Read it slowly aloud. Think
about what you just read. Read it
aloud again. Think about it some
more, concentrating on the word
saints. Talk to the Lord about what
you see in this verse.

You may be wondering what the big deal is about the word "saints." You are probably thinking, *Why should I care that Paul called the people in Ephesus saints?* Here's some background that will help you understand. The church had recently been established, and Paul was writing to encourage these believers to live in a way that brought glory and honor to Jesus. In this masterful description of the universal church, Paul begins by calling the Ephesian believers what they were: **saints**. Notice that he did not begin this letter by saying, "Paul, an apostle of Jesus, to the pathetic sinners who need to get their act together." This greeting is the exact opposite.

■ **Answer honestly: Which do you see yourself as?**

❑ sinner
❑ saint

Growing up in church, I never doubted how pathetic I was. I heard on a consistent basis that God was holy and I was a sinful creature. I was taught that without holiness, I could have nothing to do with God. I began to develop a picture of God as a furious dictator up in the sky with a gun pointed at me, waiting for me to mess up so he could shoot me. My mindset was that God took pleasure in looking down on how terribly sinful I was.

But a weird thing happened in my late 20s as I began to start really reading and studying the Bible. I discovered that when I accepted Jesus as my Savior, my identity changed. I went from being a sinner to a saint. That's right, I said it! **I am a saint of God.** At this very moment, because of Jesus' work on the cross, I am holy and blameless in God's eyes. The author of this lesson is like the early believers in Ephesus; he's a saint.

■ **How can a Christian call himself/herself a saint of God?**

_____

_____

_____

_____

It is so liberating to know that God sees Jesus in us. It brings such great joy to our hearts to know that our Father sees us as holy because we are in Christ. But even with this knowledge, we must ask the following question: *If I am a saint and not a sinner, what happens when I sin?* The church today needs to address this question. The answer is that we are saints who sin, not pathetic, hopeless sinners.

■ **What do you think you need to do when you sin?**

_____

_____

_____

_____

_____

A freeing message of the cross of Christ is that I am not identified as a sinner anymore. I know that I keep saying this, but it can't be stated enough. When I am grounded in this truth and I have renewed my mind to it over and over, I know what to do when I fall and give in to sin. Even though sin is not our master anymore, all of us know we will still fall and struggle. What the Lord wants us to do when we fall is to confess what we have done before him. There is power in confessing with your mouth what you have done. But as we confess, we should not forget to remind ourselves of our identity as saints. Doing this gets us back on the right track of following God. We will have less and less of a desire to sin when we know our true identity. If you are in Christ, you are a saint.

Today's prayer exercise may make you uncomfortable at first, but take the risk and try it. Take your Bible and find a mirror. Once you do, look in the mirror at your reflection and read Ephesians 1:1 aloud. Then read the following truths aloud: "I am a saint of God. Even though I may not feel this way, it's true. God's word is truer than my feelings, and he says that I am a saint." Let those words sink in for a minute. Then spend some time in prayer asking God to open your eyes to your true identity as a saint who sometimes sins, not a pathetic sinner who can do no right.

a loving
father

2 Chronicles 7:11-22

There's one particular day from my childhood that I will never in a million years forget. I was 14 years old, and my dad gave me an instruction: "I want you to watch your brother and sister all day long. Whatever you do, don't leave the yard. Stay here all day and keep an eye on them." He hadn't given me the most complicated instructions in the world. I understood clearly what I was supposed to do. The problem was that I didn't obey my father. My siblings and I were hanging out and playing in the living room. Then the phone rang. It was my friend Lew with an invitation I wish I had never heard. "Hey, man, we're playing softball, and we need one more. Come play ball." Now I knew good and well that I was supposed to stay at home, but for some reason, I whipped around to my brother and sister and said, "Get on your bikes kids—you're gonna watch me play some ball." Throughout the whole game, I couldn't believe what I had done. As soon as the game ended, all three of us rushed back to the house. I wanted to beat my dad back. I even prayed, "Lord, please, just this one time." I was so relieved when we got back to the driveway and I saw that my dad's car wasn't there.

Later that evening my dad said, "Thank you so much for watching your brother and sister. You're a great big brother for them." I wanted to hide under a rock for twelve years. I went back into my room and agonized over the fact that I had disobeyed my father. I sat there for two hours and finally decided that I had to confess. I walked into his room and sobbed as I spilled my guts. But my dad put his arm around me and said, "Buddy, I forgive you. By the way, I saw the three of you at the field today when I drove past. I'm proud of you for telling me the truth."

■ Have you ever confessed anything to God?
- ❏ yes
- ❏ no

If so, explain that situation. What was it like?

_____

_____

_____

■ Why do you think God wants us to confess our sins to him?

_____

_____

_____

Read 2 Chronicles 7:11-22

God gave Solomon a great promise here as he led the people of Israel. Because of promises like this one, we don't have to guess what will happen when we confess. God clearly says what he will do when we bow before him, humbly confess our sins and change our ways. When we confess, he will hear us, and he will forgive. There is no doubt about it. We don't have to wonder if God will forgive us. God is our loving Father.

My dad knew I was at the field when I was supposed to be home. He saw my brother and sister and me there and knew I had disobeyed him. He could have pulled the car over right then and whipped me in front of everyone. Even when I confessed to him later that night, he could have yelled at me and told me how pathetic I was. But he didn't. Even though my father was disappointed, he still loved me. This is such a great picture of God. When we walk away from God, we find that he doesn't walk away from us. We need only turn around to see he is right beside us. When we tell him about our sin, he's not waiting to shout, "I can't believe you did that. You're such a joke." We confess to a loving God, a God who will hear us and forgive us.

■ How do you feel when you haven't confessed a sin to God?

❑ miserable   ❑ embarrassed
❑ anxious   ❑ loved
❑ guilty
❑ other _____

■ How does it make you feel to know that you are confessing to your loving Father, not someone who is waiting to punish you?

_____

_____

_____

_____

prayer exercise:

Claim the promise God sets out in this passage today. Humble yourself before God. Confess the ways your pride gets between God and you. Pray for your needs. Seek God's face. Say "Yes" to him today. Confess your sins to him today. Thank God that he hears you. Thank him that he heals not only you but the world around you as well. Pray for your land today.

confession
and community

My family tree includes quite a few people who have struggled with alcoholism. I remember as a child being at my grandmother's house and overhearing one of my cousins talking about going to an AA meeting. I had no idea what AA was, so I asked my grandmother. She explained that AA stands for Alcoholics Anonymous, and it's a place where you can go to be with a group of people who share similar stories.

Now that I'm older, I've read about this organization and what it is about. I've discovered that what happens at an AA meeting is a picture of what confession is. A person walks into a room full of people who struggle with alcoholism, and he has the opportunity to share about his own struggle if he chooses. People all over the world have found hope and healing by going to these meetings. If you were to go, you'd hear people confess about how their sin has hurt themselves and their families. Through this time of confession in week after week of these meetings, people find the courage to beat the addiction of alcoholism. One of AA's core values is that there is power in confession—not only confession to God, but other people as well. As Christians, we can learn about the power of confession in community from AA. We too need safe places to be ourselves, confess our sins, and meet God.

■ **Have you ever confessed your sins to another person?**

☐ yes
☐ no

If so, write about that experience. If not, write about the reasons you have not done so.

_____

_____

_____

■ Why do you think the Lord wants us to confess our sins to each other?

_____

_____

_____

■ Should we confess our sins to anyone who walks by, or should we do it in the context of a solid relationship? Explain your answer.

_____

_____

_____

There is power in community. If you are not walking with Jesus in a community of believers, you don't know what you're missing. Community gives us a place to share what's going on in our lives. God doesn't intend for us to keep everything bottled up. Community provides a safe place where we can find healing as we confess about mistakes we have made and sins with which we struggle.

Reflect on the following quote:

Our brother ... has been given to us to help us. He hears the confession of our sins in Christ's stead, and he forgives our sins in Christ's name. He keeps the secret of our confession as God keeps it. When I go to my brother to confess, I am going to God.[1]

—Dietrich Bonhoeffer

■ **What do you think this quote means?**

_____

_____

_____

God is the inventor of community. One of the benefits of community is that it provides an atmosphere where God can move in mighty ways. God loves us **through other people**. Sometimes we look for God and wonder why he won't speak to us or move in our lives. If we realized that God often wants to hug us and love us through his people, we would run to community. The next time a Christian brother or sister gives you a hug, receive it as a hug from God. We need to realize what happens when we confess to a Christian brother or sister. As you do, God is there as well. Confessing to other people helps us in our spiritual formation with Jesus and points us to life as God intends it.

prayer exercise:

Write down a list of some people in your life to whom you believe you can confess. Make sure that you don't share your sin with just anyone. Whoever is on your list needs to fit the following criteria:

- ■ Can I trust this person with the confidentiality of my confession?
- ■ Is this person mature enough to handle my confession?
- ■ Will this person promise to help me overcome my struggles instead of glorifying them or making fun of them?
- ■ Would this person feel comfortable confessing to me?

If you are not currently in a community of believers, pray that God would send people your way with whom you can follow Jesus. Ask God to open your eyes to the power of community.

notes

1. Dietrich Bonhoeffer, *Life Together* (New York: Harper & Row, 1952) 112.

Isaiah 43

freedom
defined

Freedom! If you have ever seen the movie *Braveheart*, then it is hard for you to hear that word without recalling Mel Gibson's impassioned plea. There is something spine-tingling about the big cause wrapped up in this single word. We all want to be free. But what is freedom really? Is it just living however we want to live? Sometimes living life how we want to live it only puts us in greater bondage than we were before we got our freedom. The question remains: What is freedom?

■ **What do you think it means to really be free?**

_____

_____

_____

_____

■ **What are you struggling to be free from in your life?**

❑ expectations   ❑ fear
❑ guilt   ❑ sin
❑ depression   ❑ rules
❑ other _____

Read Isaiah 43

In this passage, the children of Israel find themselves in a pretty heavy predicament. After living a life of sin and refusing to listen to God, they had been captured by the Babylonian Empire and taken from their homeland. Everything they held precious had been destroyed. Many years before,

Isaiah had warned them of this possibility, but it is now a reality. They live in a different country. They are in bondage. Their place of worship back home has been destroyed. They feel abandoned by God. They know their sin had brought this calamity upon them. They are anything but free to live the life God intends for them.

The words of Isaiah 43 breathe hope into this desperate situation. The children of Israel did not need to think this was the end. Freedom was on the way. The whole chapter points to the possibility of a different way of life. Confession made this change possible. The people repented of forgetting the Lord, and now Isaiah's message of new life could be heard.

```
Fill in the blanks:
Isaiah 43:25 says, "I, even I, am he who
_____ out your _____, for my _____
sake, and _____ your _____ no more."
```

I think the power of this chapter rests in this verse. New life—life as God intends it—is possible. Why? God has a short memory of our sins and a long memory of his intentions. What a truth! God chooses to forget our sin and gives us grace for life. We need not be controlled by forces of guilt, sin, depression, expectations or fear, because our God waits to breathe new life into our desperation. With God, we are really free, for he is the freest being in the world. When we embrace the life he intends for us, living in the grace that he has provided for us in Jesus, then we are truly free.

Right now many of us need to spend some time meditating on the power of verse 25. Right now some of us are in bondage to feelings of guilt, feelings from which God has released us, which we have taken on ourselves as a kind of penance for past wrongs. Some of us are carrying loads we were never meant to carry. Jesus is calling, "Come to me, all you broken pieces. Find freedom in my sacrifice. I have paid your penalty. You are free to really live in me."

Here is a new definition of freedom: Living life as God intends it, through the grace of God, as child of God. This is the life of the Garden, and it is available to us through confession. Jesus has finished our payment for sin on the Cross. Through confession, we continue to embrace the life he so desperately wants us to have.

We have spent a lot of time this week dealing with the power of confession in our lives. In order to keep this continual opportunity central in our minds, we need to build some relationships where we are free to confess and experience God's grace. Yesterday, we talked about the power of confession in community. Continue to pray that God would send people like this into your life. If God has brought people like this to your mind over the past couple of days, approach them and risk the opportunity of confession.

This page is designed to give you space to take notes during your "Redefining Normal" group session or to journal your reflections on the highlights of this week's study.

Over the past five weeks, we've talked about the process of redefining normal. But the things we've talked about so far are the backdrop for what we believe the heart of this study is all about. Spiritual disciplines, confession, moral boundaries and a foundation of grace are key stages of the journey. But we still have far to go. To live a life of blessing, we must become people of faith, hope, and love.

The next three weeks will give us a picture of the life God intends. This leg of the journey will require us to learn new words such as risk, dance and adventure. It may require us to leave comforts, security and safe havens of Christianity to which we are so accustomed. But the journey will not disappoint. Our world needs Christians to be more than disciplined, more than moral, more than honest; our world needs Christians to be blessings. If you have the courage to redefine normal, or you want to have the courage, read on. We don't claim to have all the answers, but we are on the journey as well, following the whisper of the life God intends for us. From a few steps ahead, we can tell you it is the adventure of a lifetime.

—David Rhodes and Chad Norris

REDEFINING NORMAL

REDEFINING NORMAL FAITH

stepping into the unknown

more than
a decision

■ Write down your definition of faith.

_____

_____

_____

   Do you know that you know that you know? Are you absolutely sure? If you died in fifteen seconds are you absolutely positive that you would go to heaven? Many of us who have grown up around church have heard these questions thousands of times. Now don't get me wrong—our eternal destinies are a big deal. But I believe that questions like these leave us with an incomplete picture. Let me explain: If I think faith is only defined as a decision I make, then I am absolutely missing it. Faith is so much more than walking down an aisle or signing a card and saying, "I believe." Belief is a huge part of it, and it's important, but my belief had better be moving me somewhere. That's the heart of what we're talking about this week as we redefine normal faith. We are called to live by faith, not only to make a decision to believe.

   Al called himself a famous hiking guide, one of the best in the entire state of North Carolina. He said he knew more about hiking than just about anyone else. He owned so much equipment that he put the other hiking guides to shame. In his mind, he literally wrote the book on hiking. One day, a group of first-time hikers came into his shop. He welcomed them by saying, "My name is Al, and you won't find a better guide than me. You're so lucky to be going hiking with me. There's nothing I don't know about the trail we're hiking today." The rookie hikers felt such peace because of everything Al was saying. They believed Al's knowledge would be beneficial to them during the hike.

   But as the group made its way through the mountains, they came upon what looked like a steep and difficult path. It was narrow and covered with loose rocks, and it went up the face of an intimidating mountain. The group looked for guidance to emanate from the one who said he knew all about trails like this one, but they were shocked to see fear all over his face. One of the first-time hikers asked, "What's the problem, Al? Surely you know how we can get up this trail safely." Al was too nervous to speak. He had talked a lot about hiking and proclaimed his expertise, but he had never hiked up a trail like this one. As long as the trail was easy, he was fine. But when it became difficult and dangerous, he was out of his league. He told the group, "I don't know. I guess we'd better turn back and find another way."

Another member of the group realized exactly what was going on, that Al could talk all about hiking but had never been hiking before. She also knew, because her husband had been on the trail the week before, that there was no other way out. If they were going to reach their goal, they would have to go up this trail. So she decided she would lead the group in Al's place. She started up the trail, and the whole group followed her.

The first-timers learned a great lesson that day. Just because someone has all the right equipment and claims to be the best hiking guide around doesn't mean anything. A true hiking guide does what this woman did; step right out onto the trail and lead with actions. Making a decision on impulse to be a hiking guide simply isn't enough. You need to "walk the walk" just as much as you "talk the talk."

■ **Are people walking by faith if they talk about their walk with God but their actions don't back up their words?**

❏ yes
❏ no

Explain your answer.

_____

_____

_____

_____

■ How should our faith move us?

_____

_____

_____

Read Hebrews 11:6

■ What does it mean to earnestly seek God, as this verse says?

_____

_____

_____

We love to leave everything up to God. It's very comfortable for us to think that God does everything, and we have no role. However, the Bible paints a different picture. We have to move. We have to walk. We have to dance with God. For far too long, Christians have spent their time arguing about doctrine instead of walking by faith. The time has come for the followers of Christ to earnestly seek God and walk the journey of faith. If I say that I am a hiking guide and that I know everything about hiking but I back down when a tough trail presents itself, then I have a serious problem. It's not enough to know a lot about hiking or have all the equipment. Your walk needs to back up your talk.

■ Are you willing to move out in faith and journey onto the trails God sets before you?
- ☐ yes
- ☐ no

If so, why? If not, why not?

_____

_____

_____

_____

■ How do you know you are living by
faith? (Check all that apply)

❑ I trust God to direct me instead
of making my own plans.

❑ I follow where God leads instead
of going my own way.

❑ I trust that God's rules for life
are better than my rules.

❑ I take God at his word and act on
what I believe instead of just
talking about it.

❑ Other_____

prayer exercise:

Ask God to show you this week what
it looks like to move out in faith.
Ask him to give you the courage to
step out and live that kind of life.
Before God, commit to living with
faith that moves, not stagnant faith.

the great
adventure

Wedding days are monumental times. The commitments and vows that take place on these days will hopefully last a lifetime. It is a time of celebration, friendship, and love. Very few days in life compare to your wedding day. But the days leading up to the wedding day are far different. You will never make more decisions in your life than when you are engaged. You decide on cakes. You decide on tuxedos and dresses. You decide on who will marry you. (I mean the one who will perform the ceremony; hopefully by this point you've already found a bride or groom.) You decide where and when the wedding will take place and whom to invite. It is enough to stress any bride out for the rest of her life. Marriage is simply the years you spend recovering from planning your wedding. But there's one decision that has become easier for couples to make in recent years: the decision to throw rice or blow bubbles.

There is a movement in today's culture away from the tradition of throwing rice at weddings as the bride and groom run down to the car waiting to whisk them away to their honeymoon. Instead, bubbles now provide the atmosphere for departure in most places. This movement has been fueled by the rumor that throwing rice will kill birds. The rumor goes something like this: if you throw rice, the birds will eat the rice that is not picked up. Later, when they drink water, the rice will expand in their stomachs, and the birds will explode. Weddings throughout the world have gone from rice to bubbles in an attempt to save the birds. Funny thing is, the idea that rice makes birds explode is an urban legend. It's false. Everyone is changing wedding plans because of a faulty assumption. And even though bubble makers often refer to this urban legend on their packaging, it's not true. Birds don't explode from eating rice and drinking water. The only advantage of blowing bubbles is that there is no rice to clean up once the newlyweds drive away.

This image helps us today as we continue our journey of living a life of faith. I think it gives us a good contrast in the way many of us view the gospel. Some of us view the gospel like blowing bubbles. We like it when the gospel message lands on the surface of our lives and looks nice, but then it sometimes disappears without really making much of a lasting impact on us. But the Bible The Bible portrays the gospel differently. Like the rice in the urban legend, when we accept the gospel, it is planted inside us. As we water the gospel, it expands outside of us. Living by faith is the first step in allowing the gospel to explode from the inside out.

Read Hebrews 11-12:1

■ Write the name of every character from this passage whose story you know. Think about each of their stories, and then beside each name describe how that person walked in faith.

_____

_____

_____

_____

_____

_____

_____

_____

■ Choose two people from this passage whose stories you don't know. Look up their stories in the Old Testament and see how faith characterized their lives. (Most Bibles have notes in the text or a concordance in the back to help you find the Old Testament passage.) Record your thoughts on the next page.

_____

_____

_____

_____

_____

_____

The people listed in Hebrews 11 are not just heroes of the faith. They are what normal God followers look like. We love to call these people heroes or legends so that we won't feel bad when our lives fail to embrace the same principles as theirs. But God has different ideas for us. He wants us to set out on the adventure of faith as well. He wants us to join him in his work in our world. He wants us to run. Many times this will require us to give our lives to places and things that are not "normal." It will mean living life differently than most people. But it will mean joining God on the adventure of a lifetime right in the middle of your school, workplace, and community.

Our world is hurting today because too few Christians take God up on his offer of adventure. We would rather live second-rate lives under the status quo than really live by giving our lives away. We would rather live by sight than walk by faith. Because we are far too consumed with what others think about us, we waste away from the inside as we try to "keep up with the Joneses." God calls us to live differently, to find wholeness in a God-sized adventure.

Fill in the blanks:
Hebrews 11:4 says, "By _____ Abel offered _____ a _____ sacrifice than Cain did. By faith he was commended as a _____ man, when God spoke _____ of his offerings. And by _____ he _____ _____, even though he is _____."

I can think of no verse that gives greater testimony to the life of an individual of faith. May we all join Abel in lives that far outlive us.

Meditate on the following questions as you go through your life today: In what areas is God asking you to join him in adventure? Have you settled for a second-rate life of pursuing the same things as those in the world, or are you a person of faith?

risk
and faith

Every year there are a few days to which I look forward more than all the rest. For the past few years, one of these days has been when I've had the chance to attend a little golf tournament held in Augusta, Georgia, called the Masters. My friend's family is from near Augusta, and his family has Masters tickets. Now, you can't just go buy tickets to the Masters. Only those who have been on the list for years and years are able to buy them. Because tickets are so hard to come by, an opportunity to go to the Masters is special. I don't know how long it will be open to me, so each time I go I soak up every minute of it. The world's greatest golfers gather in Augusta to play the world's greatest golf course in the world's most prestigious golf tournament. It's the golfer's version of going to Walt Disney World.

In case you haven't figured it out, I look forward to my trip to the Masters all year long. It's one of the benchmark days for which I wait expectantly the rest of the year. So you can imagine my excitement in 2003 when I was handed not just one but four tickets to go to the Masters for a day. Talk about a gold mine—this opportunity was second only to meeting Jesus face-to-face. I had the opportunity to take three of my closest friends for the experience of a lifetime. I will never forget inviting these friends to come. All of us were pumped up as we loaded up the car early in the morning and then headed to Augusta. We felt like four-year-olds headed to see Mickey Mouse for the first time. Nothing could get us down. Even though the day started kind of cold and drizzly, we came prepared to sit gladly in the chilly rain so we could be a part of this fantastic event.

On the way there, we heard that the start of play had been delayed for a few hours. We shrugged that announcement off as a minor setback and continued our journey. Once we got to the course, we parked our car and went in for a day we knew we would remember for the rest of our lives. We rushed through the line and made our way to the sixth hole to put our chairs down at our favorite spot. But the exact moment we sat down in our chairs, an announcement came over the loudspeakers that said, "Due to inclement weather, play today is cancelled." This was the first time in twenty years that an entire day of play at the Masters had been canceled. At first it seemed like a dream—or to be more exact one of the worst nightmares ever. Gradually, reality began to sink in. We had traveled to watch a tournament, but no tournament was going to be played. It was one of the most disappointing days in each of our lives. Even as I write this story six months later, the disappointment is still very real.

I wonder if God ever feels the same way about our lives spiritually. I wonder if he is ever disappointed because we have let a little inclement weather keep us off the course. So much of Christianity is dependent on stepping out in faith that God's heart must break to see so many of us sitting on our hands. Faith challenges us to get out of the locker room and risk our lives for God's kingdom.

Read Matthew 25:14-30

■ List the three servants, how many talents they received, what they did with the talents and the master's response to them.

First servant:

_____

_____

Master's response

_____

_____

Second servant:

_____

_____

Master's response

_____

_____

Third servant:

_____

_____

Master's response

_____

_____

■ What was the master's assessment of
  the third servant?
  ☐ blessed   ☐ evil
  ☐ forgiven   ☐ so-so

■ What holds you back from the risk of
  living the life of faith in God's
  kingdom? (Check all that apply.)
  ☐ fear   ☐ laziness
  ☐ failure   ☐ careless attitude
  ☐ complacency   ☐ knowledge
  ☐ relationships
  ☐ past disappointment

This striking parable gives us a sneak peek of God's heart. Jesus shows
us that not only is God disappointed when we fail to take risks for his
kingdom, but he also says in this parable that a failure to take risks can be
sinful. We often overlook this truth in our journey with God. God is not
interested in having a bunch of fans or cheering squads on the sidelines. He
wants us to be players and expects our faith to lead us to risk our lives for
his kingdom. That doesn't necessarily mean becoming a missionary in the
most dangerous place in the world (although it could), and it definitely isn't
a call to risk only for risk's sake. Yet God wants **everything** in our lives—
our finances, our pride, our security—to be on the table as we follow him.
Jesus encourages us to get off the sidelines and into the game. This may be
scary and risky, but the life of faith cannot be lived without risk.

Meditate on the following quotes:

It is rarely counted as evil when we live in neutral (doing nothing). At worst a passive life is only pitied, yet God counts it as a tragedy when we choose to simply watch life, rather than live it. Jesus described as evil the servant who left his talent unused.[1]

Mistaking the active life of faith for an institutionally backed and culturally bound belief system is similar to reducing the Mona Lisa to paint-by-numbers.[2]

notes

1. Erwin McManus, *Seizing Your Divine Moment* (Nashville, Thomas Nelson, 2002) 44.

2. Dan Taylor, *The Myth of Certainty* (Downers Grove, IL, InterVarsity Press, 2000) 124.

Acts
6-7

what is
success?

I love the stories about the little guy who takes on the giant. Stories of an underdog get my adrenaline flowing. When I was growing up, the *Rocky* movies were popular. I loved the fact that boxer Rocky Balboa could defeat guys who were stronger, faster, and smarter than he was. I also love the stories from the Bible where the underdog shows faith in God, and God makes him or her victorious. The stories of David, Ehud, Esther, Noah, Moses, and Deborah are just a few examples. These people didn't just talk about faith; they lived by it. They dared to believe God for the impossible, and they acted on it. These stories excite me and spur me on in my walk with God. They make me want to live on the edge and trust God in all situations of life.

Even though I love these biblical heroes and heroines and I know their stories are all true, I also have to be honest. I have questions. What am I supposed to think about God when I see someone standing in faith and he seems to fail? We all must admit that often in life, the Goliaths beat the Davids. Sometimes Pharaoh doesn't listen to Moses and allow God's people to go. All of us have seen or heard about a situation where someone was standing in faith and seemed to lose. What do we make of that?

Read Acts 6-7

■ What would you say about Stephen?

❑ Stephen won.
❑ Stephen lost.

Explain your answer.

_____

_____

_____

■ How do you think success and failure
  are measured in the kingdom of God?

_____

_____

_____

_____

   I love the story of Stephen. At first glance, it seems as though Stephen lost. He believed God and stood up in faith. Much like David, Stephen walked up to face a giant—the religious leaders of his day. He did not back down one bit. He moved in faith instead of hiding behind his belief. Stephen did everything we've always been told to do, yet he was still killed. At first glance, we wonder what went wrong. But when we think about it, we discover that **absolutely nothing** went wrong. Stephen didn't lose; he was a big winner.

   The great thing about David trusting God and going to face Goliath is not that Goliath fell but that David had the courage to believe God. Trust is our gift back to God. People like Stephen and David say, "Father, I know you to be true. You are worthy of my trust, and I'll stand for you no matter what. If I am delivered, I trust you, and if I'm killed, I trust you. I'm moving with you either way." This is awesome faith. It looked as though Stephen lost, but in reality he won. Paul tells us that to live is Christ and to die is gain (Philippians 1:21). Here's the point: if we win, we win, and if we lose, we win. Realizing this helps faith well up inside you. It gives you the courage to be a Stephen.

■ Which do you think God would say
  about Stephen?
   ☐ Stephen won.
   ☐ Stephen lost.

Explain your answer.

_____

_____

_____

The massacre at Columbine High School in April 1999 is indelibly marked in the history of our country. Two students killed twelve of their classmates and a teacher before killing themselves. Perhaps the most remarkable story to come out of this tragedy is the story of Cassie Bernall. One of the gunmen put a gun to her head and asked her if she believed in God. She said, "Yes," and the gunman shot and killed her. Some people would say that Cassie lost. I would say that if you think that way, you have a distorted view of what success is. It would not surprise me to find out one day that Cassie got a standing ovation when she went to heaven for her faithfulness and courage. She is a modern-day picture of Stephen.

The challenge for most of us won't be dying for our faith; it will be living in faith. That means we must realize that, even if we are standing in faith and things don't turn out the way that they did in the story of David and Goliath, we still win. We need to realize what Shadrach, Meshach, and Abednego meant when they said they would not bow down to the king's idol even if God did not save them (Daniel 3:18). Even if the giant doesn't fall down, God intends for us to trust our heavenly Father.

prayer exercise:

Spend some time thinking about whether you are walking by faith. Would you be willing to stand like Stephen did? Ask God to develop inside of you the courage and faith Stephen had, so that you would trust and follow him no matter what the results are.

get out
of the boat

There's a picture in my office I look at every day. It depicts Jesus and the disciples on a lake in the middle of a furious storm. Eleven of the disciples are huddled together in the boat with waves crashing all around them, but impulsive Peter has gotten out of the boat and is standing on top of the water with Jesus. This is no ordinary storm. The waves are enormous, the boat is nearly tipped over from the wind and rain is blowing so hard all over the place that no one could possibly see. This picture says more than any words I could use to describe it. As I look at it I can imagine what the disciples in the boat felt—fear, doubt, terror. But there's a huge difference between Peter and the rest of the disciples. While the rest of the disciples are huddled together in the boat, Peter has gotten out of the boat to walk on water to meet Jesus. I see fear, doubt, and terror in his face, but I also see courage and hope. Jesus stands there waiting for him.

Read Matthew 14:22-32

This is my favorite story in the Bible because it's such a vivid picture. At first glance, it looks as though Peter is the one who is scared. After all, he starts to sink almost as soon as he gets onto the water. Almost every sermon I've ever heard on this passage gives Peter a hard time for his doubt and unbelief. But I see it another way. If Peter were such a coward, why was he the one walking on water while the other eleven disciples stayed in the boat scared to death? Actually, I don't see Peter as a coward at all. Instead, I see him as a man who was willing to put his money where his mouth was. He was not just a talker— he was a man who stepped onto furious waters and walked toward Jesus.

■ How did Peter show more faith than the other disciples?

❏ He told Jesus he believed in him.
❏ He got out of the boat and swam to Jesus.

☐ He got out of the boat and walked on water toward Jesus.

☐ He pulled Jesus into the boat.

☐ He refused to drop the anchor.

■ What do you think motivated Peter to get out of the boat? (Check all that apply.)

☐ love   ☐ pride

☐ faith   ☐ excitement

☐ foolishness

☐ other _____

■ Why do you think the other disciples stayed in the boat instead of going with Peter?

_____

_____

_____

Don't get me wrong: I'm not trying to elevate Peter to the place of Jesus. I don't worship Peter, and I never will. But I applaud him for having the guts and courage to walk by faith instead of just talking about it. I'm sure that all the disciples in the boat believed in Jesus. They had seen him do marvelous miracles and supernatural healings, and they knew he taught like no one else they had ever heard. But their belief in Jesus did not move them. Peter is the one who got out of the boat. Peter is the one who showed his belief.

■ Why do you think actions speak louder than words when it comes to walking by faith?

_____

_____

_____

■ **As you look at your life, do you feel like your actions back up what you believe?**

❑ yes

❑ no

Explain your answer.

_____

_____

_____

Imagine what Peter said to the other disciples later. I can just hear him saying, "Did you see that? I walked on that water just like Jesus. I've never met anyone like this Jesus." I don't know about you, but I love being around people like Peter, people who are walking out in faith. I don't have the time or energy to sit and listen to a person go on and on about God when he is not walking with God by faith. But I love to hear the stories of people who actually "got out of the boat" so to speak.

This is the life of adventure to which redefining our normal view of faith leads us. God wants us to step into the unknown. God intends for us to live as if we're walking on the water, trusting Jesus to be there with us no matter what the conditions are around us.

■ **Which is true of you?**

❑ I'm huddled up in the boat, afraid to get out.

❑ I'm walking toward Jesus.

The storms of life are coming your way. You may be in the midst of one now. Somewhere in your life, God is calling you to get out of the boat. It may at school, at work, at home, in the college you choose, or the career you move toward. We don't know what it is, but you do. The journey of redefining normal means taking the risk and stepping out of the boat, living life on what God sees instead of what you see.

Spend some time going over this passage again. Look for truths that will help you understand what it means to walk by faith. Ask the Holy Spirit to teach you as you read and meditate on this passage. Close your time by sharing what is going on in your life with your heavenly Father and telling him of your desire to walk with him in faith.

_____

_____

_____

_____

_____

_____

_____

_____

_____

_____

_____

_____

_____

This page is designed to give you space to take notes during your "Redefining Normal" group session or to journal your reflections on the highlights of this week's study.

REDEFINING
NORMAL

REDEFINING NORMAL HOPE

becoming an agent
of awakening

living an
awakened life

Living between Greenville and Spartanburg, South Carolina, is a unique experience. Upstate South Carolina is not like Los Angeles or New York. I've come to terms with the fact that I don't live in a cutting-edge place. While there are parts of my home area that are keeping up with the times, there are also some interesting places where the city life gives way to country without warning. Greenville and Spartanburg are growing and expanding so rapidly that these intersections of city and country are all over the place.

One of these places was right next to my former neighborhood, where new brick-front homes stand right next to a cemetery. The cemetery has no official entrance sign, just a circular road that makes its way through the gravesites. The intersection of city and country meant that a lot of people from my neighborhood use this road as a jogging track. Day after day, I drive by the cemetery and notice the crowds of people there walking, running and getting a workout. So many people are there in the spring, I thought a popular fitness center was selling memberships. As Jeff Foxworthy might say, "If your workout facility is a cemetery, you might be a redneck."

To be honest, this whole thing bothered me. Here the living walk, run, and enjoy life among the dead. The contrast seemed kind of inappropriate and disrespectful to me. How could someone work on life in the midst of death? How could people be motivated for fitness while being constantly reminded that for all their sweating and pain, they are fighting the inevitability of death? It just seemed strange. Then I came across this passage.

Read Ezekiel 37:1-14

Fill in the blanks:
Ezekiel 37:3 says, "He asked me, 'Son of man, can these _____ _____?' I said, 'O _____ LORD, you alone _____.'"

■ How would you answer God's question in verse 3?

_____

_____

_____

In this passage, God brought Ezekiel to a cemetery of sorts and asked Ezekiel to walk among the bones. These bones were not just any bones. They were the bones of Ezekiel's fellow countrymen. The Babylonian empire had conquered Israel and seemingly destroyed Israel's hopes, dreams, houses, worship centers, and futures. In this atmosphere, God asked Ezekiel, "Can these bones live?" Caught between real pain for his community and the real power of God, Ezekiel turned the question back to God: "O Sovereign LORD, you alone know." God then asked Ezekiel to speak to the dry bones. When Ezekiel spoke, an awakening happened. The bones connected, and an army formed.

This is the image of the awakened life—the living walking among the dead. The life of faith moves us to this intersection, but it is the life of hope that keeps us there. What is impossible with man is possible with God. Christians are those who have been awakened to life spiritually. Every day we walk among the dead. Hope is the posture we take up in this high calling.

■ Does the image of Ezekiel 37 seem odd to you?

❑ yes
❑ no

■ What parts of your life are characterized by hope?

_____

_____

_____

_____

■ How has your life been a source of
hope to those around you?

_____

_____

_____

_____

It is sad that so little of our lives today revolves around hope. As people who have everything, we rarely think we need hope. What do we have to hope for? As people who rarely risk our security by living the life of faith, we rarely cherish hope. But the truth is that, in our culture that has so much, there has never been more brokenness all around us and in us. We as Christians must reclaim hope in our lives and for our world. This week, we are going to redefine normal hope, and in doing so see how our world needs people who become agents of awakening. Life as God intends it means walking by faith and living in hope.

prayer exercise:

Think today about the civil rights movement of the 1960s. Surf the internet or go to a library to find some information about this era of American history. As you do, notice how hope played a role in this movement. Meditate on this truth and ask God to help you learn this week how to be a beacon of hope in your world.

the eyes
of hope

If you have ever been to a sporting event, you've seen him: the fan who is so into his team that he thinks it can do nothing wrong. His team never commits any fouls. He lets the referee know how badly he has missed the call whenever he dares penalize his team. His team is always on the verge of a national championship, even if its record is 1-9. His team is the best team in the history of sports, and he lets everyone know about it.

A couple of years ago, I was at my brother's soccer match in Upland, Indiana, and a person just like the fan I described was sitting right behind me. She was the mother of one of the players. In her eyes, her son could do nothing wrong. He was always in position. He was always being fouled, and he never committed any fouls. He was by far the best player on the field. I was amazed at just how biased she was. It seemed as though everything she saw was filtered through the lens of what she thought of her son. At first her bias bothered me. Couldn't she calm down a little bit? Couldn't she see that her prejudice sometimes kept her from seeing the truth? But then it hit me that maybe it could be good to be so connected to something that it affects the way you see the world.

There is a part of me that wants to be biased. I don't mean the kind of bias that keeps you from seeing the truth or the kind of bias that leaves you prejudiced. But I want bias because I want to be connected to something. I know that may not be a popular statement in a world that prides itself on standing removed from everything and putting every idea on equal ground. But there is something inside of me that wants to be so connected to something that the connection can't help but shade my view of life and truth.

There are certain attributes in life that just don't work objectively. Take love, for example. Being in love leaves you biased. You can't fall in love and keep your distance. And once you fall in love, everything you see is filtered through an unobjective perspective. Likewise, following God can't be done from a distance either. The gospel longs to affect the way we see the world and make us see it from God's perspective.

Fill in the blanks:
Jeremiah 29:11 says, "'For I know the
_____ I have for you,' declares the
LORD, 'plans to _____ you and not
to _____ you, plans to give you
_____ and a _____.'"

■ How did Jeremiah see things differently than those to whom he was writing?

_____

_____

_____

■ How does your relationship with God cause you to see things differently than those around you do?

_____

_____

_____

We spent last week pursuing the life of faith. Faith is learning to act on what God sees. This week, we seek to add hope to our faith. Hope is learning to see what God sees. In this passage Jeremiah sends a letter to the exiles. As in yesterday's passage, where the people saw hopelessness, the prophet saw hope. In one of the Bible's most quoted verses, Jeremiah demonstrated the difference between what the people see and what God sees. The people saw captivity. God saw a future.

As people of hope we become biased, seeing the world as God sees it. While some biases are detrimental, some can be to our advantage if they give us a proper perspective on God, our lives, other people, and the world.

Looking through God's eyes, we know that there is never a situation beyond his reach. In hope, we begin to see the world as God does.

■ **In what situations in your life do you need a change in perspective?**

_____

_____

■ **How would hope give you a positive outlook on those situations?**

_____

_____

_____

■ **What would it look like for God to make you a person of hope?**

_____

_____

_____

prayer exercise:

If possible, attend a sporting event today. Look for the type of fan we mentioned early in this devotion. Notice this fan's bias and meditate on how differently he or she sees the world because of it. Ask God to give you a similar connection to him. Ask God to give you the eyes of hope.

Hosea
11:1-11

the heart
of hope

I was on a flight from Austin, Texas, to Atlanta when I heard the words from our pilot that you never want to hear on a plane: "This is your captain speaking. We're turning the plane around for an emergency landing." After he assured us there was nothing wrong with our plane, he explained that one of the passengers in first class—a different world from the scrunched-up one I was in—was having some medical issues and needed to be checked out by paramedics as soon as possible. The plane took a minor detour and landed in Houston. That meant we were going to be delayed getting into Atlanta, and it meant those of us with connecting flights out of Atlanta would have to shuffle reservations and find new connections to make our final destination.

The amazing part about this flight was that I never heard one person complain about the inconvenience. Usually when a plane gets delayed or a flight gets canceled, people get anxious, angry and downright mean. But this time it was different. It seemed like everyone understood and was more than happy to do whatever was necessary to help the person in need. In the end, I think all of us were happy that the airline was more concerned about its passengers than its destination.

One of the great truths about God is that he is not some stoic being, objectively keeping the universe together. He is the biggest lover of all time. He's not removed from life, but intimately connected to life on earth and the lives of his people. God is more concerned about people than making sure everything goes flawlessly on earth. As a result, his heart is exposed every time he remembers his covenant with his people. The heart of hope is a heart of concern, the kind of concern that stems from love.

Read Hosea 11:1-11

■ In eight words or less, sum up God's message to his people in Hosea 11.

_____

_____

■ How would you describe God's heart for his people?

☐ concerned
☐ connected
☐ full of love
☐ all of the above

Hosea 11 shows us God's heart as he cries out for his people. In this passage he cries out for his people. They have turned their backs on him, but like a wounded lover (to use Philip Yancey's term) God's heart cries out for them. He longs for them to change their ways. He wants to be their God and lead them back into a life of blessing. Israel has settled for a second-rate life, but God longs to bring change for his people's future.

■ How has God changed your future?

_____

_____

_____

It's easy think about God's heart for us, but if we are going to be people of hope we must also carry God's heart for others inside of us. We have been awakened to life in Jesus. We need not go back to second-rate living ever again. We have found true peace, passion, and contentment, not in the things of this world that change daily but in the everlasting person of Christ. Now we stand in our worlds as beacons of hope, and we not only see as God sees, we feel as God feels. The person of hope longs to see others awaken to God's heart for them. This person carries a deep concern for his fellow man. In short, people of hope are people who carry God's heart wherever they go.

- Where are some places you can carry God's heart to the hurting?

_____

_____

_____

- What would being a person of hope look like in such settings?

_____

_____

_____

_____

prayer exercise:

Take out your favorite worship CD and spend some time listening to God's heart for you. As you rest in his promises and assurances, ask him to give you his heart for others. Take some time to do some strategic planning with God about how you can carry his heart to the hopeless in your normal, everyday life.

the hands
of hope

Mel Gibson talked on *The O'Reilly Factor* about his movie *The Passion* on the life of Jesus. Read what Gibson said about his reason for making the film:

> I think it's meant to just tell the truth. I want to be as truthful as possible. But when you look at the reasons behind why Christ came, why he was crucified, he died for all mankind and he suffered for all mankind, so that, really, anybody who transgresses has to look at their own part or look at their own culpability. It's time to get back to a basic message, the message that was given. At this time, the world has gone nuts, I think. Christ spoke of faith, hope, love, and forgiveness. And these are things I think we need to be reminded of again. He forgave as he was tortured and killed. And we could do with a little of that behavior.[1]

Jesus was a person of hope. He didn't just talk about hope, see hope, or feel hope. He lived hope. Throughout the gospels, we see Jesus walk into hopeless situations and bring new life. He was the ultimate example of walking as the living among the dead. He is the ultimate example of living as God intends.

Read John 5:1-15

■ What hopeless situation describes the man at the pool?
- ☐ He was mute.
- ☐ He was deaf.
- ☐ He was an invalid (lame).

■ What question did Jesus ask the man?
- ☐ "Do you want to get well?"
- ☐ "What brings you to this pool?"
- ☐ "What's wrong with you?"

The story in this passage is a powerful portrayal of hope. Jesus came upon an invalid at the pool of Bethesda. The word "invalid" used here in our English translations gives us a dual picture of this man's hopelessness, because the word can mean lame or inconsequential (not valid). This man lived for thirty-eight years in hopelessness because of his infirmity. You would have to think that so many days by the pool would have made him cynical at best. Thirty-eight years is a long time to deal with anything, much less a debilitating illness. Then Jesus entered his situation not just with a heart of hope but also with hands of hope. First, he asked the critical question, "Do you want to get well?" Jesus then healed the man and left both the man and his situation changed. Now the man was free to live as God intended.

We too walk into situations every day that need the hands of hope. While we may not be agents of physical healing all the time, we can give, help, pray and love. We too are called to be agents of blessing to the people that we meet. We must not be content to live only with hands raised to God in worship. We must be people who also extend our hands to the hurting around us. Just as Ezekiel was called to speak to dry bones, so too our ministry is to be agents of life. This may be as simple as a word of encouragement to someone in the middle of a bad day, or it could involve more sacrifice. It could mean going to lunch with someone and listening to her. It could mean volunteering some time at a soup kitchen or mission. It could even mean choosing a career as a medical missionary. There is always somewhere we can give hope to hurting people. The challenge today is not just to see what God sees or feel how God feels but also to act how God acts. We are to live with the hands of hope.

■ List three situations in which you could bring hope to hurting people. The first should be something that you could do without much sacrifice, such as a kind word. The second should be an issue that may require a little more help, maybe even a day of your time. The third should be more complex, perhaps a mission trip, or a direction in your career that you can move toward as a goal. Alongside the situations you list, explain your strategy to be hands of hope.

_____

_____

_____

_____

_____

_____

_____

Use the word "hope" as an acronym that lists some ways you can give your life to the same things to which Jesus gave of himself. Meditate on Jesus' life and use the letters to come up with four words that you sense God wants to describe your life.

H _____

O _____

P _____

E _____

Notes

1. *The O'Reilly Factor* broadcast, January 16, 2003

the
ultimate hope

As much as it pains me to say it, the 2003 Fiesta Bowl may have been the greatest college football championship game of all time. Going into the night, the defending champion Miami Hurricanes were heavily favored against the Ohio State Buckeyes, who many people felt were long on luck but short on talent. Ohio State had narrowly escaped defeat several times during the year as their offense sputtered, and now it was time to see what the Buckeyes were made of against the juggernaut from Miami.

As a huge Hurricanes fan, I anxiously waited for the opportunity to call my cousin Joe, a big Ohio State fan, to boast about the blowout I knew was inevitable. But the opportunity never came. What happened in Tempé, Arizona, that night shocked football fans across the country. Ohio State did not go quietly into that dark night. They gave the Hurricanes all they could handle. In fact, they gave them more than they could handle.

Though the Miami offense struggled against the stifling OSU defense, the 'Canes overcame costly turnovers and managed to tie the game 17-17 with a field goal at the end of regulation. It seemed as though the Hurricanes finally had some momentum going into the extra period. The first overtime began with Miami scoring a touchdown in typical Miami fashion. Ohio State had to answer to keep the game going. The Buckeyes stumbled and stared defeat in the face as they faced a fourth down and a very long fourteen yards to keep their championship dreams alive. Amazingly, the unheralded but gutsy Buckeye quarterback, Craig Krenzel, connected with receiver Mike Jenkins for just enough yardage for a first down, and Buckeye fans breathed a sigh of relief. But three plays later, they faced yet another fourth down play near the goal line. Basically, if the Buckeyes didn't get the ball in the end zone on this play, the game would be over, and the 'Canes would repeat as national champions. I thought there was no way the Buckeyes could survive two fourth downs in a row against the mighty Hurricanes.

They didn't. Krenzel's pass to Chris Gamble fell incomplete, and I erupted off my couch. The Miami players rushed the field, as did photographers and cameramen. The fireworks went off over the stadium, celebrating the end of the game. "What a game," I thought as I exulted in the victory. There was one problem, though: the game wasn't over. The Buckeyes' chances had been exhausted, but then an official dropped a yellow flag in the back of the end zone in what some people referred to as the most delayed penalty call of all time. Miami was called for pass interference, and Ohio State had new life. A few plays later, the Buckeyes tied the game up, sending the contest into a second overtime. Ohio State went on to pull off the upset 31-24 in double overtime to win the national championship.

The few seconds between the dropped pass and the dropped flag must have seemed like eternity for Ohio State fans. Miami was celebrating its victory. It looked like hope was gone for the Buckeyes. But in a moment, their destinies changed.

Read 1 Thessalonians 4:13-5:11

■ In what did Paul tell the Thessalonians to take hope?

_____

_____

■ Why is resurrection important to us as Christians?

_____

_____

_____

Fill in the blanks:
First Thessalonians 4:13 says,
"Brothers, we do not want you to be
_____ about those who _____
_____, or to _____ like the
rest of men who have no _____."

Paul wrote his first letter to the Thessalonians at a time of great need within their community. The Thessalonians were being persecuted for their faith, and these new converts had little external support in trying times. In the midst of that struggle, Paul encouraged the Christians in Thessalonica to live lives pleasing to the Lord. His encouragement came in a couple of forms. One was the hope about which you just read. Paul encouraged the Thessalonians that even death was not the end of the game for them. Even though death seemed final, resurrection would get the last word on their lives. They did not need to be sorrowful as those who had no hope, because death was not the end.

This week, we have been talking about embracing the life of hope. We have been challenged to live with God's eyes, God's heart, and God's hands. As we do so, we, too, should find encouragement in the fact that we have the ultimate hope of resurrection. Death no longer has the last word on our lives or on our work in this world. As Christians we know that the game extends far past our death, not because of a yellow flag but because of the magnificent work of Christ. We, too, will join in his resurrection. Although at times it may look as though evil has triumphed, the fireworks are going off and the victory pictures are being taken, the game is not over. The hope that drives us to live the life God intends for us on this earth also climaxes with life after this world. We live with the hope of resurrection on our minds and in our hearts.

prayer exercise:

Think back to the last time that you were at a funeral. Imagine the scene, smell the smells, hear the music. What emotions did you feel? Now remember that for Christians death is not the end. Even in death new life is being embraced. Live in this ultimate hope today.

_____

_____

_____

_____

_____

_____

_____

_____

_____

_____

_____

_____

_____

_____

_____

   This page is designed to give you space to take notes during your "Redefining Normal" group session or to journal your reflections on the highlights of this week's study.

REDEFINING NORMAL

REDEFINING NORMAL LOVE

the life God intends

God is
love

This statement may seem a little extreme, but I believe that a person's greatest hindrance in his walk with God is a distorted picture of who God is, especially when it comes to love. So many people have been deeply scarred because they didn't comprehend our heavenly Father's love. It's very common for people to think that God is distant, mad, and angry, looking for any opportunity to pour out his wrath. Although it is true that he will judge the world, he does not want anyone to perish (2 Peter 3:9). His heart is open wide to give you love. He is patient, kind, good, gentle, mighty, and caring. If people really knew how loving God is, they wouldn't hesitate running to him. He truly is all we need.

Read 1 John 4:13-18

■ Do you ever wonder whether God really loves you?

❑ yes
❑ no

What does this passage say about God's love?

_____

_____

_____

_____

■ Do you have a hard time accepting God's love for you?

❑ yes
❑ no

If so, why do you think you have trouble accepting God's love? What would you say to others who are struggling in this area?

_____

_____

_____

_____

In my own personal journey, God has opened my eyes to see what his love is all about. I spent most of my life wondering if he really, truly loved me. I could quote Scriptures all day long about his love, but I never really felt it. But one night after I preached to a group of students, I went backstage, fell to my knees and told God, "All I've ever wanted to know is that you love me." That was three years ago. Since then, God has taken me on a journey of love too amazing for words. No amount of pages are enough for me to express what God has shown me. Let me just say this: Satan will do anything he can to blind you to what God really thinks about you. Colossians tells us that the enemy loves to deceive, and one of the greatest deceptions he uses with Christians today is this issue of God's love.

Focus on these truths: There is **no** condemnation for those who follow Christ Jesus (see Romans 8:1). God is not furious. He is **pleased** with you if you live for Christ Jesus. God's wrath will be poured out one day, and those who are not following Christ will experience his judgment. But those of us who have surrendered to Jesus have **nothing** to fear.

Read Luke 15:11-31

■ What does this story tell us about our heavenly Father?

_____

_____

_____

- Why do you think so many believers have a distorted view of who God is?

- What is the remedy to this problem?

- How can we renew our minds to the love of God?

People tend to go to extremes, even when it comes to talking about God. Some people see God as a cute teddy bear that is loveable but docile and powerless. Others see God as an ogre. But a balanced view depicts God as a mighty king who rules the entire universe but has a tender and compassionate heart. What an awesome concept! God is not a powerless, stuffed animal, nor is he a ruthless dictator. God is a loving Father who desires to love you and receive love from you. He wants to show you who he is. Before we can redefine normal love, we must be rooted in grace and the knowledge of who God really is. As we begin to understand this truth, we will wake up to the life God intends.

prayer exercise:

Take some time to write God a letter. Express your love for him and your questions about him, and ask him to show you his love for you. After you are finished writing, take time in silence to listen to God. Give him space to tell you how much he loves you.

love
yourself

Today's topic is one about which I've never heard a sermon preached. Could you imagine going to church and hearing a sermon entitled "Love yourself"? This is something many of us don't often think about. Because we have such a tendency to be self-absorbed and selfish, we don't think we have any trouble loving ourselves. But when you really think about it, you can be selfish and self-absorbed and still hate yourself. When most people start evaluating themselves spiritually, they realize they don't like what they see at the core of who they are. It's easy for us to think about what it means to love others and serve God, but it's difficult to ponder how we can love ourselves. Obviously, we need to make sure we keep a balance, because God doesn't want us to be narcissistic (in love with ourselves); however, he wants his children to accept themselves and think of themselves as he thinks of them.

Read Romans 5:1-11

The cross is God's ultimate expression of his love for us. Even though we had walked away from him and chosen sin, he ran to us, sending his son to die for our sins. If God loves us this much, it must break his heart when we don't value ourselves. Loving ourselves is not about being in love with ourselves, it's about seeing ourselves as God sees us. Blaise Pascal said, "God made man in his own image and man returned the compliment."[1] We often think God sees us as we see ourselves. But when we don't love ourselves, that's not true. God loves us, and that means we are worth loving.

Reflect on this quote:

I hope it is clear that feelings of guilt, accompanied by anxiety, fear and restlessness, arise from deep within ourselves and are not an accurate gauge of the state of our souls before God. We cannot assume that he feels about us the way we feel about ourselves, unless we love ourselves intensely and freely.[2]

■ Do you agree with this quote?

❑ yes
❑ no

Why or why not?

_____

_____

_____

■ What feelings do you have when you look at yourself?

❑ guilt and shame   ❑ love
❑ anxiety   ❑ restlessness
❑ thankfulness
❑ other _____

■ How can you move toward seeing your-self and loving yourself as God sees you and loves you?

_____

_____

Amy almost never missed going to church on Sundays and Wednesdays. She became a Christian at age seven and doesn't have many memories of her life before Christ. As long as she can remember, she has been reading her Bible, praying, and practicing other spiritual disciplines. Amy is so dedicated that she won't go to bed without having a quiet time, no matter what time it is. Somewhere along the way, she got the impression that God would get very angry with her if she failed to do "Christian things" like doing devotions and going to church. This belief, combined with her perfectionist tendencies, caused her to be consumed with doing these things without fail.

But when Amy started the 11th grade, she hit the wall. Amy told her parents she felt like she just wasn't good enough and that God was disappointed in her. Amy's father couldn't believe what he was hearing, because Amy had her act together more than most adults. Still, Amy continuously beat herself up about what she wasn't doing and how much she disappointed God. Guilt, shame, and remorse were her constant companions. Amy figured following God meant living this way.

Then one summer day, Amy was in the backyard. It was an ordinary day, and Amy was laying out by the pool, enjoying the sunshine, when she heard somewhere deep inside her, "Amy, I love you so much." It caught her so off-guard that she figured it must have been her mind playing tricks on her. But then she realized that she never would have thought anything like that about herself. After a few moments, a calm came over her. She knew beyond a shadow of a doubt that God had spoken to her. She realized she had been going about following God with the wrong motivation, that God didn't want her to follow him out of fear. In the days and weeks that followed, she started to read the Bible and began to see how the Lord talks about his people. She was learning that God loved her and that she could love herself. Amy became more patient with herself, and she even learned to be gentle and forgiving as she dealt with her shortcomings.

■ Have you ever tried to please God to the point of exhaustion only to realize that you were being too hard on yourself?

❑ yes
❑ no

If so, explain that situation. If not, how have you avoided this trap?

_____

_____

_____

_____

_____

Spend some time evaluating whether you are too hard on yourself. Talk to the Lord and ask him to help you be gentler with yourself. Start looking at yourself the way your God looks at you. To do so, you may even want to read 1 John and allow the truths of that book to sink deeply into your soul.

notes

1. Blaise Pascal, *Pensees* (New York: Dutton, 1958) 58.

2. Bernard Bush, *Coping with God* (Whitinsville, MA: Affirmation Books, 1976) 28.

our
ultimate aim

I will never forget my first visit as a parent to the pediatrician's office. In case you don't know, a pediatrician is a children's doctor. The pediatrician's office is not somewhere you would normally go to hang out. It's not a fun place to spend an afternoon. But when you are a parent, there's no way to avoid taking your child to the pediatrician's office at least occasionally.

The first time I walked into our pediatrician's office, I knew I was in a different world. Slobbering babies, screaming two-year-olds and rambunctious toddlers waited in the healthy section to see their doctor for a check-up. And that was the pleasant part. The sick section of the waiting room was filled with runny noses, loud coughs, and just about every smell there is. As I sat there, I felt like I was one breath away from catching the flu. When we walked back to see our pediatrician, one particular room caught my attention. In the back corner of the office in Room 5, it sounded as though something horrific were taking place. A little boy was screaming, "No mommy! Please mommy! Don't let them do it to me mommy!" Then came a piercing scream that got everyone's attention. I chuckled a little bit as I asked a nurse what was going on in there. She assured us that everything was OK. The boy was getting his vaccination shots. Because he had been there before, he recognized what would happen when he went into Room 5, and he wanted no part of it.

I asked the nurse if the shots were really necessary, and she explained to me about the need for certain vaccinations. Basically, vaccinations are shots pediatricians give children to make sure they don't come down with certain illnesses. A vaccination shot puts a little bit of a virus into the child, and the child's immune system then builds up an immunity to that virus, protecting him from the illness the virus causes. In other words, to keep a child from getting measles, a pediatrician shoots a little bit of measles into the child so that his immune system will defeat the virus and the child won't have to worry about getting measles for the rest of his life.

In a similar way, many of us have become vaccinated to the gospel. By being around it so much, we have built up immunity to it and made sure that it doesn't take over too much of our lives. We want a belief system and a free pass to heaven, but we don't want the gospel to spread over into the rest of lives. But God has different ideas. He wants an epidemic of love of biblical proportions to break all over our lives and all over our world. When God's love fully infiltrates our lives, it leads us to this epidemic of love.

Read Mark 12:28-34

■ What does Jesus say is the greatest commandment?
- ☐ Love God.
- ☐ Hope in God.
- ☐ Have faith in God.

■ What does Jesus say is the second greatest commandment?
- ☐ Love yourself.
- ☐ Love others.
- ☐ It's a trick question; there is no second part.

In Mark 12, the Pharisees cornered Jesus. They wanted to discredit him as a teacher, so they asked him a couple of tough questions intended to trap him no matter what his answer was. But time after time, Jesus confounded them with his wisdom. Finally, a teacher in the law asked Jesus the question they had all been waiting to hear. Let's put his question into modern vernacular: "If you could narrow following God down to one thing, what would that one thing be?" Jesus' answer is stunning. I expect him to say faith, because faith is what Jesus looked for throughout the pages of the gospels. Or I expect him to repeat one of the Ten Commandments and tell us not to kill or lie. But Jesus doesn't answer negatively; he answers with **love**—telling us to love God and love other people.

The love Jesus described here is not the kind of love most of us think about when we hear the word. It is not the kind of love found on TV reality and dating shows. It is a love whose greatest desire is not to get but to **give**. Jesus calls us to respond to God and our world with the same kind of love God gave to us.

■ Which word best describes your life
  over the past year?

☐ jealousy   ☐ patience   ☐ anger
☐ gossip   ☐ passion   ☐ brokenness
☐ bitterness   ☐ pain   ☐ persistence
☐ love   ☐ envy   ☐ pleasure

■ What would it look like for love to
  become the description of your life?

_____

_____

_____

prayer exercise:

Watch one of the many TV reality
shows that revolve around love
today. Notice how shallowly love is
portrayed in these shows and how
much the shows focus on getting.
Then meditate on God's love for a
moment. Notice how much God's love
focuses on giving. Ask God to help
you understand love the way he
understands love. Then journal what
you sense him saying to you today
in the space provided below:

_____

_____

_____

love
others

John 13:1-17

■ If you had to draw a picture of what love looks like, what would you draw?

_____

_____

There has never been anyone who demonstrated what love looks like better than our Savior, Jesus Christ. All you have to do is follow him through the gospels to see what love is. Some people are experts when it comes to talking about love, but others show it. Jesus loved to extend love to those around him. After his resurrection, he went to a beach near where some of his disciples were fishing. They looked to the shore and saw their Savior making breakfast for them. Think about it: Jesus was serving them breakfast, even after all of them had scattered and deserted him. This is such a great picture of Jesus demonstrating love. Today, we're going to look at another great picture.

Read John 13:1-17

It's amazing to see God in the flesh on bended knee washing dirty, disgusting human feet. Jesus showed his disciples the full extent of his love with a humble act of service. He once again went beyond talking about what to do to show us what love really entails.

■ What, if anything, is odd about what Jesus is doing in this passage?

_____

_____

■ What does Jesus tell his followers to do in verse 14?

☐ Encourage each other.
☐ Carry each other's burdens.
☐ Wash each other's feet.

When I was a freshman in college, I went to Romania on a mission trip. I really did not know what to expect while I was there, but I was excited to go. We were there for a couple of weeks taking part in different ministry opportunities. It was a trip I will never forget, one of those life-changing experiences that will affect me from now until I get to heaven. When I got back to the United States, a pastor friend of mine asked me what I thought about the trip. I told him, "When I went over there, I expected to serve and love on the Romanians. What I was not prepared for was the unbelievable servanthood and love they showed us." I have never been around a group of people who acted more like Jesus in my life. They served our group the entire time we were there. You can learn and experience more things of Jesus on a trip like that than you can by reading one hundred books. To see someone love you the way Jesus does is amazing. The trip made me want to live that way. I've got a long way to go, but I learned during that time that God takes joy when his children serve and love each other.

■ In what ways do you think loving and serving others makes you more like Christ? List as many as you can.

_____

_____

_____

_____

_____

_____

It's easy to think about our own needs. Most of us get so busy with what is happening in our own lives that we fail to reach out and love and serve other people. But when we fall into that rut, we miss out, because there is joy in loving and serving others. God says it is better to give than to receive, and that's true when it comes to love. Showing the full extent of our love for God and others means giving our lives away to people in service.

■ Do you serve other people in your life?

❏ yes
❏ no

If so, why do you serve? How do you serve? If not, why not?

_____

_____

prayer exercise:

Think about one person to whom you can write a note of encouragement today. Don't write just to do the right thing or to finish the devotion; write from your heart. Express your love and appreciation to that person. Try to think of another person whom you can serve and love in whatever way God lays on your heart. You may want to wash that person's car, help with chores or take that person out to eat. Ask the Holy Spirit to put people on your mind who need to be loved today, and give your love away.

back to
the diving board

When we started our journey of redefining normal, we began with the picture of the diving board. We talked about our tendency to be paralyzed by the thought of messing up, to be content with "pencil dives" when God is calling us to flips and "gainers." Over the last eight weeks, we have marked out the life God intends for us. Now, as we come to the end of this study, we stand once again atop the high dive, ready to leap off. Still, the drama remains. Will we risk the life of **"Yes"** or remain in the life of **"No"**? Will we become people of faith, hope, and love, or will we continue to measure our Christianity merely by the things we don't do? Today God is calling you to the life he intends for you.

Read 1 John 4:7-21

Fill in the blanks:
First John 4:16-17 says, "And so we know and rely on the _____ God has for _____. God is _____. Whoever lives in _____ lives in _____, and _____ in _____. In this way, _____ is made _____ among us so that we will have _____ on the day of _____, because in this _____ we are _____ him."

■ Put verses 19-20 in your own words using eight words or less.

_____

_____

■ How many times does the word "love" appear in today's passage?
- ☐ 1-5
- ☐ 6-10
- ☐ 11-15
- ☐ 16-20
- ☐ 21-25
- ☐ More than 25

The life of blessing is what we have been journeying toward in this book. We have learned that God has great hopes for our lives beyond our salvation experiences. His greatest hope is that we would be people of love. In a world that throws the word "love" around flippantly, we as Christians are to embody real love for God, others, and our world. This will require risk, faith, hope, community, passion, crucifixion, and mission, as we've talked about throughout this study. But we must not turn back. When we love, we become God's ambassadors to his world. We become a part of the re-creative work he is doing. We play a role in changing our world.

Today, a cry must go out for people from many different places to be part of a revolution, the revolution of love John talks about this in 1 John 4. We can no longer be content only to talk about following God. If we are not loving our brothers and sisters, and if we are not loving our world, then we are not loving our God. We love to talk about love. We often give ourselves the credit for loving God more than we actually do. But John's word is convicting. We know we love God if we love our brother.

This book has been a radical call to redefining normal in our lives. We have showed you the way, but we cannot make you begin the journey. Only you can risk the flips and gainers God has in store for you. Come and join those who have gone before us, the community of saints who are jumping into the pool. It is time to do a "one-and-a-half" and dive in headfirst.

- How has God called you to redefine normal in your life over the past eight weeks?

_____

_____

_____

_____

prayer exercise:

Spend some extended time in prayer today asking God to help you redefine normal in your own life and help you become an agent of redefining normal in the lives of others. Ask God to help you be a blessing to our world. Ask him to continue to show you life as he intends it. Conclude your prayer time by reading the following verse and asking God to make it true of you: "We continually remember before our God and Father your work produced by faith, your labor prompted by love, and your endurance inspired by hope in our Lord Jesus Christ" (1 Thessalonians 1:3). As you leap, jump, and dive, know that we are praying this prayer for you as well.

This page is designed to give you space to take notes during your "Redefining Normal" group session or to journal your reflections on the highlights of this week's study.

REDEFINING NORMAL
About the Authors

CHAD NORRIS

Chad is a speaker and writer who desires to lead people in their spiritual journeys to become loving followers of Jesus Christ. In this calling, he speaks to children, students, and adults in a variety of settings and writes several resources. Chad is a co-founder of Wayfarer  Ministries and serves as one of the weekly teachers for Engage, a praise and worship Bible study for 20-some-things in upstate South Carolina. After graduating from the University of Georgia in 1995, Chad received his Master of Divinity from Beeson Divinity School in 2000. Chad's love of the journey and realistic view-points help nurture people in their personal spiritual growth. This is the third book Chad has co-authored in the Following God for Young Adults series. Chad, wife Wendy, and son Sam live in Greer, SC.

DAVID RHODES

As a speaker and author, David has a passion to help people rediscover life as followers of Jesus Christ. His creative, challenging, and honest approach encour-  ages a variety of individuals and groups in various min-istry settings. David is a co-founder of Wayfarer Ministries and one of the weekly speakers at Engage, a praise-and-worship Bible study for 20-somethings in upstate South Carolina. David graduated from Palm Beach Atlantic University in 1996 and earned his Master of Divinity from Beeson Divinity School in 2000. This is the third book David has co-authored in the Following God for Young Adults series. David, wife Kim, and daughter Emma live near Greenville, SC.

For more information about the authors of this study, please contact:
Wayfarer Ministries
1735 John B. White Sr. Blvd.
Suite 9, Box 201
Spartanburg, SC 29301-5462
www.wayfarerministries.org